Gordon Ramsay

Quick and Delicious

Gordon Ramsay

Quick and Delicious

Delicious

**100 Recipes to Cook
in 30 Minutes or Less**

GRAND CENTRAL
PUBLISHING

NEW YORK   BOSTON

Grand Central Publishing
Hachette Book Group
1290 Avenue of the Americas, New York, NY 10104
grandcentralpublishing.com
twitter.com/grandcentralpub

Originally published as a hardcover in Great Britain in 2019 by Hodder & Stoughton, a Hachette UK Company. Hodder & Stoughton Ltd, Carmelite House, 50 Victoria Embankment, London EC4Y 0DZ

First Grand Central Publishing Edition: September 2020

Grand Central Publishing is a division of Hachette Book Group, Inc. The Grand Central Publishing name and logo is a trademark of Hachette Book Group, Inc.

The publisher is not responsible for websites (or their content) that are not owned by the publisher.

The Hachette Speakers Bureau provides a wide range of authors for speaking events. To find out more, go to www.hachettespeakersbureau.com or call (866) 376-6591.

Editorial Director: Nicky Ross
Project Editor: Natalie Bradley
Editor: Camilla Stoddart
Copy-editor: Patricia Burgess
Design and Art Direction: Peter Dawson, Alice Kennedy-Owen, gradedesign.com
Photographer: Louise Hagger
Food Stylist: Nicole Herft
Prop Stylists: Alexander Breeze and Louie Waller

Library of Congress Cataloging-in-Publication Data has been applied for.

ISBNs: 978-1-5387-1-9336 (hardcover); 978-1-5387-1932-9 (ebook)

Printed in the United States of America

WOR

10 9 8 7 6 5 4 3 2

Contents

Introduction

Speed is a vital ingredient in restaurant kitchens: it is essential to get the food out quickly, or people just won't come back. Although things are less pressured at home, there is a lot to learn from professional chefs when it comes to getting great food onto the table quickly. Personally, I never cut corners when it comes to flavor, but there are many tricks that I've learned over the years for saving time while cooking. In this book, I share this knowledge and my experience to help you produce amazing meals fast. Every recipe can be cooked in roughly thirty minutes (we all move at different speeds, so there is a bit of give-and-take here), and, in my opinion, each one punches above its weight. What I mean by this is that the quality and tastiness of the finished dishes far outweigh the amount of effort put into cooking them. This is quick and easy food without compromising flavor in any way.

I know that modern life is busy and tiring, and that it's getting easier and easier to order takeout or have prepared meals delivered to your home. But where's the satisfaction and pride in opening the door to a man in leathers and a helmet? And where's the pleasure and sense of achievement in pricking the plastic wrap of a prepared meal before sticking it in the microwave? Cooking from scratch is better for you, much less expensive, and so much more satisfying than buying dinner in. And it needn't take long to produce incredible food for yourself and your family. In fact, by the time your limp, sweaty takeout has made it from the restaurant to your house, you could have made any of the knockout dishes in this book and be tucking into properly great food.

Producing restaurant-quality meals in half an hour can be a challenge. The time constraint rules out many of the techniques that chefs rely on to bring depth of flavor and complexity to a dish—marinating, braising, roasting, and slow cooking, for example. But there are ways around this if you know how: choose the right ingredients, marry them with the right combination of spices and sauces, use the right cooking method, and you can produce incredibly tasty meals that tick all the boxes. Quick food doesn't mean bland and one-dimensional, especially when you bring in an arsenal of aromatic spices and condiments from across the globe (see pages 6–7). In fact, being short of time forces you to be more creative in the kitchen, not less.

When I'm at home, I don't want to spend hours cooking, but I still want to eat well. The recipes in this book are some of my go-to dishes when time is short but the appetite for something delicious is strong. Using bold flavors and some clever labor-saving cheats, I know I can produce top-quality food in under thirty minutes. If you follow the tips and techniques in these pages, you too will become a faster and better cook with a bigger repertoire of no-nonsense dishes from around the world. And by being well prepared, choosy about your ingredients, and more efficient in the kitchen, you will be able to produce incredible food in no time at all. Shouldn't you be cooking already?

Gordon x

My Advice for Faster, Better Cooking

Clear the decks

The state of your kitchen before you start cooking will make a big difference in how you cook. Starting with a clean work surface, a sink clear of washing up, and an empty dishwasher will help everything run more smoothly. A tidy kitchen leads to much better efficiency and, therefore, better food.

Switch off distractions

There's a reason that my chefs aren't allowed to use their mobile phones during service.... Producing an amazing dish in a short space of time requires concentration and focus. I know that life can get in the way, but your cooking will be more successful if you give it your full attention.

Read the recipe before you start

I'm sure you've heard this piece of advice before, but how often do you actually follow it? It might seem like a waste of time when you're keen to get food on the table, but I can't emphasize enough how much time you will save if you do this. You will know exactly what to expect, what you need to prep in advance, and which pieces of equipment you will need and when. Nothing is more frustrating than hunting for a whisk when you're halfway through a recipe.

Get your equipment out

Before you start, know that you can easily lay your hands on all the kitchen equipment you need to complete the recipe. Get your scale/food processor/blender/mandoline out of the drawer or cupboard so you won't waste valuable minutes trying to find them. And sort out any jobs, such as lining a baking sheet or setting up a bain-marie, at the outset. It will allow for a much smoother, stress-free process.

Get your mise en place in place

Getting all the ingredients ready before you begin will also save time once you start. Measure what you need to, and gather all the spices, sauces, and seasonings that you'll need. Reading the recipe through before you start means that you'll know what prep you will need to do up front, and what you can leave for a suitable time in the process. For example, all the ingredients for a stir-fry need to be ready before you start, whereas the garnish for a soup can be prepped while the soup is cooking.

Buy the best

Professional chefs know that the secret to good cooking is actually good shopping. If you buy great ingredients, whether that's organic, well-aged meat, fruit and veg in the right season, or super-fresh seafood from a fishmonger, you are more than halfway there before you even start cooking. This is especially important when it comes to producing meals in a short space of time—the tastier the produce, the less you have to do to it to make it sing.

Take shortcuts

When time is short, I'm all for cutting a few corners, such as buying pre-chopped butternut squash from a supermarket, or using pre-cooked rice. We don't think twice about buying canned tomatoes or beans, or jars of roasted peppers and artichokes, so why not use other unadulterated ingredients that have been prepped or cooked for you? I draw the line at store-bought sauces and flavorless stock cubes, but if the ingredients haven't been messed about with in any way, feel free to save yourself a bit of time—especially if it means you are more likely to cook from scratch than resort to prepared meals or takeout.

Clean up as you cook

It is good practice to tidy up as you go along. Keep a waste bowl next to your cutting board for the rubbish you create as you prep fruit and veg; that way you only need to make one trip to the bin at the end, rather than several time-wasting trips throughout. It keeps the work surface clear too. Chefs always wipe down their stations between tasks, and it's great to get into this habit. Fill a sink or washing-up bowl with warm soapy water so you can immediately put dirty pans and spoons in it (never put sharp knives in, as they can cause accidents). Also, load the dishwasher as you go along. By the time you finish cooking, the washing up will virtually be done and it won't feel like a bomb has exploded in the kitchen.

Sharpen your knives

It is essential that your kitchen equipment is in good condition. This is especially important when it comes to knives—a blunt knife is not only more dangerous; it is also seriously inefficient. Sharpen your knives before you start and every time you cook. It will make all the difference to prep times.

How to sharpen a knife

Hold the steel confidently in your non-dominant hand and use your other hand to place the heel of the knife (where the blade meets the handle) on top of the steel near its own handle. Draw the knife along the steel in a sweeping motion so that you stroke the entire length of the blade against it, keeping the angle between the steel and the blade at a steady 20 degrees. Now hone the other side of the knife by placing the blade under the steel and repeating the motion. Do this five or six times, alternating the side of the blade with each stroke, until you have a sharp edge. The more you do this, the quicker you will become.

Practice your knife skills

Chefs don't just hone their knife skills so they can look good chopping at speed on TV. They become good at wielding that knife so they can chop 10 pounds of onions in half the time it would take anyone else. Learn to use your knives like a professional and you too will speed through your veg, meat, and fish prep. Take a course or watch online tutorials, then practice what you've learned every time you chop anything. Using your knife confidently and ergonomically will make you a faster, more effective cook.

Harness the heat

When you're trying to cook something quickly, it can be tempting to get it into the oven straight away, but if the oven hasn't had a chance to get up to the right temperature, it will take longer to cook and it will be more difficult to work out when to take it out again. Likewise, if you don't wait for a grill pan to be smoking hot before you add your chops, it will take much more time to get a good color on the outside of the meat, by which time the inside will be overcooked. Always wait for the oven to come up to temperature, for frying pans to be hot enough, and for water to be actually boiling before you add any pasta or vegetables. Your food will thank you for it.

Equipment List

Good cooking isn't dependent on having a kitchen full of gadgets. There are, however, a few pieces of equipment that will really help you to get delicious food onto the table in less time. Here is my list of essentials, starting with the most important.

Good knives

You can do almost everything with just three knives—a large chef's knife, a small paring knife, and a serrated bread knife. Keep them sharp (see page 3), store them well (i.e., in a knife block or on a rack rather than loose in a drawer), and always wash them by hand. Follow these rules and your knives should last for years.

Blowtorch

Blowtorches aren't just for browning the sugar on top of a crème brûlée. We use them all the time in my kitchens to char the marinade on meat or fish, to melt cheesy toppings, and to caramelize sugar on all sorts of desserts. They take seconds to use and should be part of any speedy cook's arsenal.

Digital scales

Not only are they more accurate than old-fashioned kitchen scales; digital scales are also much faster to use. You can weigh all the ingredients straight into the measuring bowl, using the tare function to return the display to zero before each one. They're great for weighing liquids too.

Food processor

A food processor makes light work of jobs such as shredding cabbage or celeriac, grating cheese, puréeing soup, and making fresh breadcrumbs. Use the smaller bowls for blitzing small amounts and whipping up dressings, marinades, and sauces.

Grater

Whether you favor a good old-fashioned box grater or a fancy Microplane, some sort of grater is essential for quickly grating a little bit of cheese, mincing a piece of ginger, or zesting a lemon.

Mandoline

However good you are with a knife, a mandoline is incredibly useful for fast, uniform slicing. I use one repeatedly in this book because it is such an efficient way to slice beets, carrots, cucumbers, apples, and such without having to get the food processor out.

Mortar and pestle

A large, heavy mortar and pestle is a great piece of kitchen equipment for pounding and grinding herbs and spices, unleashing their flavor without totally pulverizing them.

Speedy peeler

The clue is in the name—a swivel peeler will make light work of peeling fruit and veg, and as it removes only the skin or outermost layer, you are left with more of the flesh. It's also great for shaving hard cheeses and for quickly slicing veg into ribbons.

Stick blender

A stick blender is so useful for quickly blitzing hot soups, dips, and dressings on the spot. You can also use it for making smoothies, bringing batters together, and whipping cream.

Silicone baking mat

Lining a baking sheet with a silicone mat takes literally seconds and there are no burning issues as with parchment paper. You can also use them over and over again, which is much better for the environment than aluminum foil and parchment paper.

Shortcuts to Flavor

When time is short, seasoning is vital, as there isn't time to develop the deep flavors associated with roasting, braising, and slow cooking. It's therefore important to keep a well-stocked pantry. Having an array of different sauces and spices will mean you are never far away from a quick, tasty meal. I am assuming that you have olive oil, some sort of vegetable or sunflower oil for frying, some vinegars, mustard, and salt and pepper, as well as a collection of herbs and spices, but here is a list of ingredients you might not already have that are guaranteed to liven things up.

Dashi powder

Dashi is Japanese stock made from the seaweed kombu, which is rich in umami and forms the base of many Japanese dishes, from miso soup to ramen noodle broths. Powdered dashi is the quickest way to inject that savory richness into your cooking.

Fennel pollen

An intense, anise-flavored spice from the flowers of the fennel plant, this is great sprinkled over fish, chicken, pork, and salads.

Fish sauce

A stalwart of East and Southeast Asian cooking, fish sauce is a fermented condiment that brings a savory umami hit to dipping sauces, noodles, soups, and stir-fries.

Furikake seasoning

A tasty mixture that typically contains black and white sesame seeds, dried seaweed, and dried fish. The Japanese use it mostly for sprinkling over rice; it can also be used to instantly pep up fish, chicken, and rice dishes.

Gochujang chile paste

Fermented chile paste from Korea that is sweet, savory, and very hot all at the same time. Brilliant in marinades and sauces, it can also be stirred through stews, stir-fries, and soups.

Harissa

A fragrant chile and red pepper paste from North Africa that is used to flavor meat, couscous, stews, and sauces. Rose harissa is a fragrant variation in which the rose petals temper the chile and add a gentle sweetness.

Lemongrass paste

All the fragrant intensity of fresh lemongrass in a very useful paste.

Mirin

A sweetened rice wine from Japan that is a bit like saké. It is used to add a sweet tang to dipping sauces, broths, and marinades.

Miso paste

Japanese fermented soyabean paste that is packed with umami. It can be white, yellow, red, or simply dark, depending on how long it has been fermented, with white being the mildest and red being saltier and stronger.

Paprika

Can be hot, sweet, smoked, or unsmoked, but whichever type you use, paprika will add an instant smokiness and depth to your food.

Ras-el-hanout

A Moroccan spice mix that instantly transports you to the souks of North Africa, this is an easy way to add an exotic taste to rubs, marinades, and tagines.

Time-Saving Ingredients

Rice vinegar
A mild, slightly sweet vinegar used to bring a subtle acidity to sauces, marinades, and stir-fries.

Saffron
The mild spice that brings a golden yellow color and subtle but distinct aroma and flavor to sauces, risotto, pasta, fish, and chicken dishes.

Shaoxing rice wine
A fermented rice wine that gives depth and complexity to Chinese sauces and soups.

Shichimi togarashi (seven-spice powder)
A tasty blend of seven spices, including chile flakes, orange peel, sesame seeds, and ground ginger; it is used to brighten up soups, noodle dishes, grilled meat, and fish.

Sichuan peppercorns
A lip-tingling pepper-like spice that adds a fragrant punch to Chinese cooking.

Sriracha sauce
Thailand's versatile chile sauce, which is hot and tangy with a gentle sweetness.

Sumac
A citrusy spice popular across North Africa; it can be sprinkled over dishes to add the sharpness of lemons and limes.

Tamarind paste
Adds an instant sweet-and-sour note to sauces and marinades.

Thai shrimp paste
A paste that imparts the strong salty taste of fermented shrimp and adds body to Southeast Asian curries and noodle soups.

It isn't cheating to buy pre-prepped ingredients—it's like having a secret sous chef in your pantry and a junior chef in the freezer! But make sure that the ingredients you buy have just been chopped or cooked rather than adulterated in any way. Here's a list of things to buy to help speed up your cooking.

- Frozen chopped chiles, onions, and herbs
- Frozen peas and spinach
- Pre-chopped veg, especially those that are tricky to peel, such as butternut squash and pumpkin
- Spiralized vegetables
- Cauliflower "rice"
- Cooked beets
- Bags of salad greens
- Canned tomatoes, beans, and lentils
- Roasted peppers and artichokes
- Crispy fried onions
- Fresh pasta and noodles
- Pre-cooked rice
- Prepared pastry (puff pastry and piecrust)
- Breadcrumbs, dry and fresh
- Fresh stock

Soups and Salads

Cauliflower Soup with Brown Butter and Cheesy Toasts 13

Chicken and Shiitake Noodle Soup 14

Celeriac and Apple Soup with Crushed Walnuts 17

Spiced Squash and Lentil Soup 18

Soba Noodle, Zucchini, and Shrimp Salad with Tamari Dressing 21

Kale Caesar Salad with Garlic Croutons 22

Warm Eggplant, Tomato, and Burrata 25

Halloumi, Asparagus, and Green Bean Salad 26

Beet Salad with Whipped Goat Cheese 29

Vietnamese Meatball Noodle Salad 30

Cauliflower Soup with Brown Butter and Cheesy Toasts

Serves 4

2 tablespoons olive oil
1½ tablespoons butter
1 onion, peeled and finely chopped
2 garlic cloves, peeled and sliced
Small handful of sage leaves
1 (2-pound) cauliflower
2 cups chicken or vegetable stock
¾ cup whole milk
1 cup heavy cream
Sea salt and freshly ground pepper

For the brown butter
3 tablespoons butter
1 tablespoon truffle oil
Handful of sage leaves

For the cheesy toasts
4 slices of baguette, thinly sliced
  on the diagonal
4 ounces grated cheese mixture
  (mozzarella, Cheddar, blue, and
  Gruyère, or a combination of
  whatever you have in the fridge)

Time-saving tip
If you warm the stock in a
saucepan over medium heat
while you prep the onions, garlic,
and cauliflower, it will come to
a boil quicker when you add
it to the soup pan, therefore
speeding up the whole process.

Making brown butter, or _beurre noisette_, is one of those techniques that chefs love but home cooks seem to steer clear of because it sounds tricky. Believe me, it's really not complicated, and the more often you do it, the more confident you become at judging the right time to take the pan off the heat. It's such an easy way to add a rich nuttiness to this creamy soup, and it smells incredible.

1 Preheat the broiler.
2 Place a large saucepan over medium heat and add the oil and butter. When the butter has melted, add the onion and garlic and cook for 5 minutes. Add the sage leaves and cook for 1 additional minute.
3 Meanwhile, prepare the cauliflower by removing the leaves and separating the florets. Roughly chop them into small pieces of the same size.
4 Add the chopped cauliflower and the stock to the pan. Season with salt and pepper, bring to a boil, and simmer for 5 minutes. Add the milk and cream and simmer for an additional 8 minutes.
5 Meanwhile, make the brown butter. Put the butter into a small saucepan and place it over high heat. When it begins to brown, remove the pan from the heat and add the truffle oil and sage leaves. Stir well and leave to cool.
6 Now make the toasts. Lay the baguette slices on a baking sheet and broil for 2–3 minutes, until lightly golden on one side. Turn each slice over, then sprinkle liberally with the grated cheese. Place under the broiler again for an additional 4 minutes, or until the cheese is melted and golden.
7 When the cauliflower is cooked, blend the mixture with a stick blender until smooth. Check the seasoning and adjust as necessary. Ladle the soup into bowls and spoon over the brown butter and sage leaves. Serve with the cheesy toasts on the side.

Chicken and Shiitake Noodle Soup

Serves 4

1½ quarts chicken stock
4 chicken thighs, skin on
12 dried shiitake mushrooms
¾–1-inch piece of fresh ginger,
   peeled and julienned
1 star anise
2 spring onions, trimmed and
   cut in half
⅓ cup Shaoxing rice wine
6 ounces egg noodles
2 tablespoons soy sauce
7 ounces choy sum
Sea salt and ground white pepper

To serve
3 ounces bamboo shoots
Asian microgreens or cilantro leaves
2 teaspoons sesame oil

Time-saving tip
Peel ginger with a teaspoon—
it takes less time than using
a knife and there is less waste.

I love the different broths and noodle soups you find across countries such as China, Japan, Malaysia, and Vietnam. The broths for these soups are usually labored over for many hours to give them an intense depth of flavor, but this soup uses dried shiitake mushrooms to shortcut the process. They are really rich in umami, bringing a wonderful savoriness and depth to the dish in no time at all.

1 Place a saucepan over high heat. Pour in the chicken stock, then add the chicken thighs and mushrooms.

2 Add the ginger to the pan along with the star anise, spring onions, and rice wine. Season with a big pinch of sea salt and a small pinch of white pepper.

3 Bring the soup to a boil, skimming off any impurities that might rise to the surface. Once boiling, reduce the heat to a strong simmer and cook for 10 minutes.

4 Meanwhile, bring a kettle of water to a boil. Pour into a clean saucepan over high heat and season with salt. Add the noodles and cook for 3–4 minutes, until just tender. Drain the noodles and hold them under cold running water until cool. Drain again and set aside until needed.

5 Remove a chicken thigh from the broth and check if it is cooked through by piercing the thickest part with the tip of a sharp knife; the juices should run clear with no pinkness. If cooked, remove all the chicken pieces and the mushrooms from the broth and set aside.

6 Using a slotted spoon, remove the star anise, ginger, and spring onions from the broth and return it to high heat. Add the soy sauce and taste for seasoning.

7 Roughly chop the choy sum into 2½-inch lengths, and separate the stalks from the leafy parts. Add the stalks to the saucepan and allow to cook for 2 minutes.

8 Remove the skin from the chicken thighs and shred the meat, discarding the bones.

9 Add the choy sum leaves to the broth and turn the heat off.

10 Divide the noodles among four bowls and top with the shiitake mushrooms and chicken, then ladle over the broth. Garnish with the bamboo shoots and microgreens and a drizzle of sesame oil.

Celeriac and Apple Soup with Crushed Walnuts

Serves 4–6

2 tablespoons olive oil
1 onion, peeled and roughly chopped
1 celeriac (about 1½ pounds), peeled
    and diced
2 Cox's or other sweet-tart apples,
    peeled, cored, and roughly chopped
1 tablespoon thyme leaves
1 quart vegetable stock
Sea salt and freshly ground black
    or white pepper

To serve

Large handful of walnuts, roughly
    chopped
Extra virgin olive oil, for drizzling

Celeriac makes the most delicious creamy soup even without adding any cream or milk (great for vegans), but it can be very rich. Adding sweet but tart apples, such as Cox's, cuts through the richness and complements the flavor beautifully. I also love the contrast between the smooth, creamy texture of the soup and the crunchy walnuts.

1 Place a large saucepan over medium heat and add the olive oil. When hot, add the onion with a pinch of salt and cook for 4–5 minutes, until soft but not colored.

2 Add the celeriac, apples, and thyme leaves and cook for 5 minutes.

3 Pour in the vegetable stock and bring to a simmer. Continue simmering for 5 more minutes, or until the celeriac is tender.

4 Remove the pan from the heat and use a stick blender to blend thoroughly. Season with salt and pepper, then taste and add more seasoning as necessary.

5 Ladle into warm bowls, scatter with the chopped walnuts, and drizzle with some extra virgin olive oil before serving.

Spiced Squash and Lentil Soup

Serves 4

1 tablespoon light olive oil
3 tablespoons butter
1 onion, peeled and diced
1 teaspoon cumin seeds
4 garlic cloves, peeled
1-inch piece of fresh ginger,
    peeled
2 red chiles, seeded if you want
    a milder hit
1 teaspoon mild curry powder
2 pounds butternut squash
1¼ quarts chicken or vegetable stock
1⅓ cups red lentils
1 cup coconut cream
Sea salt and freshly ground black
    pepper

To garnish

2 tablespoons light olive oil
1 teaspoon cumin seeds
Large handful of fresh curry leaves
½ teaspoon mild curry powder
1 red chile, seeded if you want
    a milder hit, thinly sliced

Time-saving tip

For a really quick and easy way
to peel lots of garlic cloves, put
them into a metal saucepan with
a tight-fitting lid and shake the
pan really vigorously with both
hands for about 30 seconds,
or until all the garlic cloves are
miraculously peeled. This also
works for a whole bulb!

Soup is the ultimate fast food, and this hearty meal-in-a-bowl is a great example—it is nourishing, warming, and filling and takes only half an hour to rustle up.
I usually make a double batch and freeze it for an even quicker meal down the line. Suddenly winter evenings don't seem so dark and cold! Use vegetable stock to make this soup vegan.

1. Heat the oil and butter in a large saucepan over medium heat. When the butter has melted, add the onion and cumin seeds and cook for 2–3 minutes.

2. Meanwhile, place the garlic, ginger, and chiles in a small food processor and blend to a paste. Add this to the pan along with the curry powder and cook for another 2–3 minutes.

3. Prepare the squash by peeling the skin off and removing all the seeds with a spoon. Cut the flesh into ½-inch cubes and add to the pan together with the stock. Increase the heat to high and bring to a boil.

4. Add the lentils and cook for 10 minutes.

5. Put the coconut cream into a small bowl and whisk until smooth. Reserve 6 tablespoons for the garnish and add the rest to the pan. Cook over high heat until the squash is soft and the lentils are cooked.

6. While the soup is cooking, heat the oil for the garnish in a small frying pan. When hot, add the cumin seeds, curry leaves, and curry powder. Stir well, then remove the pan from the heat.

7. Using a stick blender, blend the soup until smooth, then season with salt and pepper and ladle into individual bowls. Drizzle over the reserved coconut cream and the curry oil. Sprinkle with a few slices of red chile before serving.

Soba Noodle, Zucchini, and Shrimp Salad with Tamari Dressing

Serves 4

7 ounces soba noodles
Peanut oil, for drizzling
7 ounces spiralized zucchini
   (about 2 zucchinis)
5 ounces cooked shrimp
5 ounces cherry tomatoes, halved
1 ounce chives, finely chopped
2 tablespoons sesame seeds

For the tamari dressing
½ teaspoon Dijon mustard
1½ tablespoons rice vinegar
1 tablespoon sesame oil
2 tablespoons tamari soy sauce
1 tablespoon mirin
¼ cup olive oil
¾-inch piece of fresh ginger,
   peeled and grated
1 garlic clove, peeled and crushed
Pinch of sea salt

This Japanese-inspired noodle salad is packed full of flavor and bite. You can spiralize your own zucchini if you have a spiralizer and time on your hands, but these days you can buy "zucchini noodles" from some supermarkets. Alternatively, use a mandoline or julienne grater to shred the zucchinis before adding them to the noodles. Be wary of adding too much salt to the dressing, as soba noodles and tamari soy sauce contain plenty already.

1   Bring a kettle of water to a boil, then pour it into a large saucepan. Return to a boil over medium-high heat, then add the soba noodles and cook for 4 minutes. Drain and rinse under cold water to cool the noodles quickly. Drain thoroughly, then drizzle with a little peanut oil to stop the noodles from sticking together.

2   Put the cooled noodles into a large bowl and add the spiralized zucchini, shrimp, tomatoes, and chives.

3   To make the dressing, put all the ingredients into a bowl and whisk to combine.

4   Toast the sesame seeds in a dry frying pan for 2–3 minutes, until golden, shaking the pan regularly.

5   Pour the dressing over the salad and toss well to ensure that all the ingredients are well coated. Scatter over the toasted sesame seeds before serving.

Kale Caesar Salad with Garlic Croutons

Serves 4

1 large garlic clove, peeled and
  crushed
3 tablespoons olive oil
2 tablespoons finely chopped flat-leaf
  parsley
4 slices sourdough bread
1 tablespoon vegetable oil
7 ounces smoked bacon, cut into
  1-inch strips
3½ ounces mixed kale (green and
  purple, if available)
4 heads Little Gem lettuce
3½ ounces cremini mushrooms, thinly
  sliced
½ red onion, peeled and thinly sliced
8 anchovies in olive oil (optional)
1½ ounces Parmesan cheese
Sea salt and freshly ground black
  pepper

For the dressing
½ cup good-quality French
  mayonnaise
1 large garlic clove, peeled and
  crushed
¾ ounce Parmesan cheese, finely
  grated
1 teaspoon Dijon mustard
Juice of ½ lemon
8 anchovies in olive oil
1–2 tablespoons water

You can't escape kale these days: it crops up in scrambled eggs, smoothies, and pasta sauces, on pizzas, even in cakes and brownies—pretty good for a once deeply unfashionable type of cabbage! Tana and I have embraced these dark leafy greens in our house, as she loves kale and tries to sneak it into the kids at every opportunity. I, on the other hand, think it makes a great addition to a classic Caesar salad, but don't let it anywhere near my brownies!

1   Preheat the oven to 400°F. Line a baking sheet with parchment paper.

2   Put the garlic, olive oil, and parsley into a bowl, season with salt and pepper, and mix well.

3   Tear the sourdough into small pieces and put them into the bowl with the garlic oil. Mix until well coated, then spread the bread over the prepared sheet. Place in the oven and toast for 8–10 minutes, until golden brown.

4   Place a large nonstick frying pan over medium-high heat. When hot, add the vegetable oil, then the bacon and cook for 5–8 minutes, until crispy.

5   Meanwhile, make the dressing: put the mayonnaise, garlic, Parmesan, mustard, and lemon juice into a bowl. Chop the anchovies, add to the bowl, and stir to combine. Add the water to loosen the dressing.

6   Tear the kale into bite-sized pieces. Trim the lettuce and separate the leaves. Cut the larger leaves in half lengthwise and keep the smaller leaves whole. Put all the leaves into a salad bowl with the sliced mushrooms and red onion.

7   Pour the dressing over the salad and toss well. Scatter over the croutons and bacon, then cut the remaining anchovies in half lengthwise and lay them on top (if using). Using a vegetable peeler, shave the Parmesan over the salad before serving.

Warm Eggplant, Tomato, and Burrata

Serves 4

3 eggplants, trimmed and sliced
   ½ inch thick
¼ cup olive oil
2 pounds heirloom tomatoes, sliced
   ½ inch thick
3 ounces arugula leaves
3 balls burrata
Sea salt

For the dressing
¼ cup olive oil
1 shallot, peeled and thinly diced
2 garlic cloves, peeled and finely
   diced
3 rosemary sprigs, leaves picked and
   finely chopped
3 tablespoons red wine vinegar
½ teaspoon chile flakes (optional)
Freshly ground black pepper

I know chefs are always banging on about how much the quality of the ingredients matters, but it's absolutely true that if you source the best produce, more than half the work is already done before you even get into the kitchen. That truth is never more apparent than when it comes to an uncomplicated salad like this one… there is nowhere to hide. Make sure you use sweet, ripe tomatoes and firm eggplants in season, then splash out on really good-quality, creamy burrata and you can't go wrong.

1   Place a grill pan over high heat.
2   Brush each eggplant slice with a little of the olive oil and sprinkle with salt. Lay a few of the slices, oil side down, on the grill pan, brush the tops with a little more oil, and sprinkle with a little more salt. Cook for 2–3 minutes on each side until charred and soft. Repeat with the remaining slices.
3   Pour the oil for the dressing into a small saucepan and place over medium heat for 2–3 minutes. It is hot enough when a piece of shallot added to the pan sizzles gently. Turn the heat off, then add all the shallot, the garlic, and the rosemary and mix well. Leave to cook gently for 2–3 minutes, then add the vinegar and chile flakes (if using) and season with salt and pepper.
4   Layer the eggplant slices and tomatoes in a shallow bowl or on a platter. Drizzle each layer with a little of the dressing, then sprinkle with the arugula. Cut each burrata in half and place on top. Drizzle with the remaining dressing and serve.

Halloumi, Asparagus, and Green Bean Salad

Serves 2

9 ounces green beans, trimmed
3½ ounces asparagus, trimmed
9 ounces halloumi cheese
½ teaspoon chile flakes
1 tablespoon olive oil
7 ounces cherry tomatoes, halved
2 ounces pitted Kalamata olives
Small handful of pea shoots
Sea salt and freshly ground black
    pepper

For the dressing
2 basil sprigs, leaves picked
2 mint sprigs, leaves picked
1 tablespoon red wine vinegar
3 tablespoons extra virgin olive oil

Time-saving tip
To trim green beans in no time at
all, line them up in the bag so that
all the woody ends are together,
then use a chef's knife to cut
through the plastic and trim all the
beans in one go.

You can keep unopened halloumi for up to a year in the fridge, so you are never more than half an hour away from a cracking summer lunch like this one. I love the combination of asparagus, green beans, tomatoes, and olives, but you can replace these, or add to them, with whatever you have in the fridge on the day: avocado, cucumber, edamame, mixed salad greens, and grilled zucchini all work well.

1 Bring a kettle of water to a boil, then pour it into a saucepan. Season with salt and place it over high heat. Once boiling again, add the green beans and cook for 4 minutes, then add the asparagus and cook for an additional minute. Drain and place the vegetables in a large bowl of iced water to stop the cooking process.

2 To make the dressing, put the basil and mint leaves into a small food processor with the vinegar and oil. Season with salt and pepper and blend until smooth.

3 Cut the halloumi in half horizontally so you have two rectangles. Sprinkle each one with some of the chile flakes.

4 Place a nonstick frying pan over medium-high heat. When hot, add the oil and gently swirl it to coat the base evenly. Put the halloumi slices into the pan, chile side down, and sprinkle the top with a little more chile. Cook for 2–3 minutes on each side, until golden brown.

5 Meanwhile, drain the green beans and asparagus and put into a bowl with the cherry tomatoes and half the dressing. Mix well and divide between two plates. Place the halloumi on top.

6 Add the olives to the frying pan to warm through, then sprinkle them around the halloumi. Drizzle with the remaining dressing and garnish with a few pea shoots before serving.

Fish
and
Shellfish

Fish Finger Sandwiches

Serves 2

10 ounces haddock or cod fillets

¼ cup all-purpose flour

1 egg

1 tablespoon whole milk

½ cup panko breadcrumbs

1 tablespoon chopped dill

2 ciabatta or brioche rolls

Vegetable oil, for frying

Large handful of watercress

Sea salt and freshly ground
black pepper

For the tartar sauce

¼ cup good-quality French
mayonnaise

1 shallot, peeled and finely diced

4 cornichons, finely chopped

2 teaspoons nonpareil capers

1 tablespoon finely chopped flat-leaf
parsley

Lemon juice, to taste

Chef's tip

Before coating the fish in the panko,
rub the breadcrumbs through your
fingers to make sure they are all the
same size—they will cook much
more evenly.

What I really want to achieve in this book is to show you how quick and satisfying producing food from scratch can be and how much more delicious it is than a prepared meal. This fish finger sandwich is a case in point. Yes, you could bung some frozen fish fingers in the oven and open a jar of store-bought tartar sauce, but it wouldn't taste even half as amazing as this fish finger sandwich. Try it and you'll see what I mean.

1   Cut the fish into 4 equal "fingers" and season both sides with salt and pepper.

2   Set out three shallow bowls. Put the flour into one and season with salt and pepper too. Put the egg and milk into another bowl and lightly beat together. Put the breadcrumbs and dill into a third bowl and mix well.

3   Dust the fish in the flour, shake off any excess, then dip into the egg mixture, making sure all the sides are coated. Finally, cover in the breadcrumbs. Transfer to a plate and place the fish fingers in the fridge.

4   Preheat the broiler to medium-high.

5   Make the tartar sauce by mixing all the ingredients together with a little salt and pepper.

6   Cut the rolls in half and put them on a baking sheet, cut side up. Place under the broiler for 1–2 minutes, until golden and toasted.

7   Place a frying pan over medium-high heat and add a ½-inch depth of vegetable oil. When hot, shallow-fry the fish fingers for 2–3 minutes on each side, until crisp and golden all over. Remove from the oil and drain on paper towels, then season each one with a little salt.

8   Spread the tartar sauce on the bottom half of each bun. Put the fish fingers on the tartar sauce, then top with the watercress before putting the lids on to serve.

Pan-Fried Salmon with Pink Grapefruit Hollandaise

Serves 4

4 (7-ounce) salmon fillets,
  skin on and pinboned
1 tablespoon mild olive oil
1 pound asparagus, trimmed
½ cup water
2 tablespoons butter
1 teaspoon pink peppercorns
Pink grapefruit wedges, to serve
  (optional)

For the pink grapefruit hollandaise

¼ cup dry white wine
⅓ cup white wine vinegar
1 small shallot, peeled and finely
  chopped
2 tarragon sprigs, roughly chopped
14 tablespoons butter
2 egg yolks
1 tablespoon pink grapefruit juice
1 teaspoon pink grapefruit zest
1 tablespoon thinly sliced chives
Sea salt and finely ground black pepper

I know hollandaise sauce has a reputation for being tricky to make, but if you take your time when you add the butter and don't let it get too hot, you can produce an amazing, restaurant-quality sauce in your own kitchen. The tart grapefruit cuts through the buttery richness of the sauce and gives it a very slight pink blush that looks stunning with the salmon and pink peppercorns.

1   Start by making the hollandaise sauce: put the wine, vinegar, shallot, and tarragon into a small saucepan and heat until reduced to about 2 tablespoons of liquid. Strain, discarding the solids, and set aside until needed.

2   Melt the 14 tablespoons butter over gentle heat and carefully pour the golden liquid into a pitcher, discarding the milky solids at the bottom of the pan.

3   Place a heatproof bowl over a pan of simmering water. Add the egg yolks, grapefruit juice and zest, plus half of the reduced vinegar. Whisk until frothy and thick, then slowly add the melted butter, whisking constantly. Stir through the chives, then season with salt and pepper and add a little warm water if it's too thick. Add the remaining vinegar reduction if you prefer a bit more tang. Set aside.

4   Score the skin on the salmon fillets, then brush with the olive oil and season on both sides with salt and pepper. Place a large nonstick frying pan over medium-high heat and, when hot, add the salmon, skin side down. Reduce the heat to medium-low and cook for about 5 minutes, until the skin is quite crisp. Flip over and cook the other side for 2–3 minutes, until slightly springy to the touch. Remove and allow the fish to rest for a few minutes.

5   Meanwhile, put the asparagus into a large sauté pan with the water, butter, and a little salt and pepper. Place over high heat and cook for 5 minutes, or until tender.

6   Put a salmon fillet on each serving plate and place some asparagus alongside. Spoon the hollandaise over the salmon and sprinkle with a few pink peppercorns. If you wish, serve with a wedge of pink grapefruit on the side.

Moules Marinière with Wild Leek Toasts

Serves 2

2¼ pounds mussels
2 tablespoons olive oil
2 shallots, peeled and finely diced
1 large garlic clove, peeled and finely
 chopped
½ cup dry white wine, such as
 Muscadet
½ cup heavy cream
Large handful of wild leek leaves,
 finely chopped
2 tablespoons butter

For the wild leek toasts

10 tablespoons butter, softened
Handful of wild leek leaves, roughly
 chopped
4–6 slices of baguette (sliced on
 the diagonal)
¾ ounce Parmesan cheese
Sea salt and freshly ground black
 pepper

Chef's tip

If you have more wild leeks than
you need, make double the butter
recipe, roll it into a log, and freeze
it for future use. It's delicious
melted onto a steak or stirred
through risotto, and can be
used to make the Wild Leek
Turkey Kievs on page 81.

**Mussels are one of my favorite shellfish—they
are cheap, healthy, and delicious, need minimal prep,
and you can cook them in minutes. This version of
the classic French dish uses the subtle wild leek
leaves that can be foraged in woodlands in early
spring, or found at farmers' markets or from specialty
suppliers. If you can't get your hands on wild leeks,
double the amount of garlic in the liquor and add
a crushed garlic clove to the butter for the toasts.**

1 Preheat the broiler to medium-high.
2 Wash and debeard the mussels, then drain in a colander.
3 Place a large stock pot that has a tight-fitting
 lid over medium heat and add the oil. When hot,
 add the shallots and cook for 2–3 minutes, until
 softened. Stir in the garlic and cook for 1 minute, then
 add the wine. Simmer until the wine reduces by half.
4 Meanwhile, to make the wild leek butter for the toasts,
 put the 10 tablespoons butter into a small food processor
 with the roughly chopped wild leeks and a little salt and
 pepper. Blend until well combined. Set aside.
5 Add the cream and finely chopped wild leeks to the wine
 mixture, increase the heat to high, and let it reduce by
 half.
6 Meanwhile, put the baguette slices on a baking sheet
 and place under the broiler for 2 minutes, until golden
 and toasted on one side. Remove from the broiler, flip
 each slice over, then spread thickly with the wild leek
 butter. Using a fine grater, grate the Parmesan directly
 over each slice of baguette until evenly coated, then broil
 for 2 more minutes, until golden brown.
7 Add the mussels to the wine pan and stir well. Put the
 lid on and cook for 4–5 minutes, until all the mussels
 have opened. Discard any that haven't opened, then
 stir the 2 tablespoons butter into the sauce and serve
 immediately with the wild leek toasts.

Baked Halibut with Borlotti Beans and Tomatoes

Serves 4

1 pound cherry tomatoes

2 (14-ounce) cans of borlotti beans, drained and rinsed

4 (7-ounce) halibut fillets, skinned

Pinch of chile flakes

2 garlic cloves, peeled and thinly sliced

1 tablespoon nonpareil capers

2 rosemary sprigs, leaves finely chopped

1 unwaxed lemon, thinly sliced

½ cup dry white wine

3 tablespoons olive oil

12 ounces Broccolini

½ cup water

2 tablespoons butter

Sea salt and freshly ground black pepper

Small handful of basil leaves, to serve (optional)

You can't beat a one-pan dinner for ease and speed, and a meaty fish like halibut is perfect for the job. The tomatoes and wine will ensure the fish doesn't dry out while cooking, and everything in the pan will absorb all the lovely flavors of the lemon, rosemary, and garlic, making this a super-tasty midweek supper that will go down a storm with all the family.

1 Preheat the oven to 425°F.

2 Put the tomatoes and borlotti beans into a roasting pan and season with a little salt and pepper.

3 Season both sides of the fish with salt and pepper and place them on top of the beans and tomatoes. Sprinkle the fish with chile flakes, then scatter the garlic, capers, and rosemary over everything in the pan. Put the lemon slices on top, then pour over the wine and drizzle with the olive oil.

4 Place the pan on the top shelf of the oven for 12–15 minutes, until the fish is cooked through.

5 Meanwhile, place the Broccolini in a large sauté pan with the water and butter. Season with salt and pepper and cook for 5 minutes, turning halfway through for even cooking.

6 When the halibut is cooked, sprinkle with the basil leaves and serve with the Broccolini and crusty bread.

Scallops with Creamed Corn and Pancetta

Serves 2

7 ounces green beans, trimmed

1 tablespoon olive oil

8–10 scallops, with roe attached (if available)

1 tablespoon butter

Sea salt and freshly ground black pepper

For the creamed corn

3 ounces pancetta, finely diced

1 tablespoon olive oil

1 onion, peeled and finely diced

2 ears corn on the cob

2 garlic cloves, peeled and finely chopped

½ teaspoon paprika

¾ cup heavy cream

2 thyme sprigs, leaves picked

⅓ cup water

2 tablespoons freshly grated Parmesan cheese

¼ cup sour cream

2 tablespoons flat-leaf parsley

Time-saving tip

If you are really in a hurry, use canned unsweetened corn instead of fresh corn kernels and reduce the cooking time by 5 minutes.

Corn, bacon, and scallops make an incredible combination—sweet, salty, and extremely satisfying. The scallops cook very fast, so wait until the last minute before cooking them. I always add them to the edge of the pan in a clockwise direction, starting at 12 o'clock, so by the time you have put them all into the pan, it's time to turn the first ones that went in. It's a simple technique for ensuring that all the scallops cook evenly.

1 Start by making the creamed corn. Place a small, nonstick frying pan over medium heat. When hot, add the pancetta and cook for 2–3 minutes, until the fat begins to render.

2 Meanwhile, place a saucepan over medium-high heat and add the oil. When hot, add the onion and cook for 5 minutes, or until softened.

3 Remove the corn kernels from the cobs by standing each cob upright and running a sharp knife down the sides. Add a handful of the corn to the pancetta pan and cook for an additional 2–3 minutes, until the pancetta is crispy and browned.

4 Add the garlic to the onion and cook for 1–2 minutes, then add the paprika, cream, thyme leaves, water, and remaining corn. Stir well and cook over medium heat for 10 minutes, or until the corn has softened and the sauce has thickened.

5 Meanwhile, cook the green beans in boiling salted water until tender. Drain and set aside until needed.

6 When the corn has softened, stir through the Parmesan, sour cream, and chopped parsley and remove from the heat.

7 Pour the olive oil over the scallops, season with salt and pepper, and gently mix until well coated. Place a large nonstick frying pan over medium-high heat. When hot, carefully add the scallops and cook for 1–2 minutes on one side, then flip over, add the butter to the pan, and cook for an additional minute. Baste the scallops with the butter and remove the pan from the heat.

8 Spoon the creamed corn into shallow bowls and add the green beans. Top with the scallops and sprinkle with the pancetta and corn mixture before serving.

Squid and Fennel Stew

Serves 4

3 tablespoons extra virgin olive oil, plus extra for drizzling

1 onion, peeled and diced

4 garlic cloves, peeled and thinly sliced

1 small fennel bulb, trimmed and thinly sliced

½ teaspoon chile flakes

2 teaspoons fennel seeds

1 teaspoon sweet smoked paprika

3 rosemary sprigs, leaves finely chopped

½ cup dry white wine

1 (28-ounce) can diced tomatoes

1½ pounds cleaned squid, or a mixture of cleaned squid and peeled shrimp

2 (14-ounce) cans of lima beans, drained and rinsed

¾ cup pitted Kalamata olives

Small handful of flat-leaf parsley, roughly chopped

Sea salt and freshly ground black pepper

This Mediterranean-style one-pot stew is crammed with flavor despite being so quick and easy to put together. Get your fishmonger to clean and prep the squid, or buy it prepared from a supermarket to reduce the amount of work you have to do to get dinner on the table. Serve it with fresh or toasted baguette to soak up the incredible sauce.

1 Place a large nonstick sauté pan over medium-high heat. When hot, add the oil and onion and sauté for 2–3 minutes. Add the garlic and sauté for 2 more minutes. Add the sliced fennel, chile flakes, fennel seeds, paprika, and rosemary and cook for 3–4 minutes.

2 Increase the heat to high, add the wine, and let it reduce by half before adding the tomatoes to the pan. Bring to a simmer and cook for 10 minutes.

3 Meanwhile, prepare your squid. Cut down the long side of each squid tube and open it out flat. Using a sharp knife, lightly score the inside of the flesh, then cut into 2- to 3-inch pieces.

4 Add the squid to the pan and cook for 5–6 minutes, stirring occasionally.

5 Add the lima beans and olives and cook for an additional 2–3 minutes. Season to taste, remove from the heat, and stir in the parsley.

6 Spoon the stew into warm bowls, drizzle with extra virgin olive oil, and serve with crusty bread and a simple salad.

Miso-Glazed Cod

Serves 4

5 tablespoons white miso paste

2 tablespoons mirin

1½ tablespoons sugar

1 tablespoons soy sauce

1-inch piece of fresh ginger, peeled
and finely grated

4 (7-ounce) cod fillets, skin on and
pinboned

12 ounces Broccolini, trimmed

1 tablespoon olive oil

For the cucumber pickle

1 cucumber

¼ cup rice vinegar

1 tablespoon superfine sugar

Large pinch of salt

To serve

Pickled ginger

2 tablespoons furikake seasoning

Japanese white miso has a wonderfully deep, savory richness and makes a great glaze for fish like cod and salmon. In the not too distant past, it was available only in Asian shops or from specialty sites online, but these days it can be found in most supermarkets. You can use it to flavor soups or poaching broths, salad dressings, stir-fries, or marinades, so keeping some in the fridge can be the starting point for many meals.

1 Preheat the oven to 450°F.

2 Combine the miso, mirin, sugar, soy sauce, and ginger in a shallow dish just big enough to hold the four pieces of fish. Coat both sides of the fish in the marinade, then leave it to marinate, flesh side down, for 10 minutes.

3 Meanwhile, place the Broccolini on a small baking sheet in a single layer, drizzle over the olive oil, and toss to coat.

4 To make the pickle, use a mandoline or food processor to slice the cucumber into very thin rounds. Place them in a bowl, add the rice vinegar, sugar, and salt, and mix well. Leave to sit for 10 minutes.

5 Put the fish onto a small baking sheet and place on the top shelf of the oven along with the sheet of Broccolini and cook for 15 minutes.

6 Remove the fish from the oven. If there are any areas where the glaze hasn't browned, run a blowtorch over the surface until evenly colored.

7 Drain the cucumber and plate the cod with the Broccolini and a spoonful of pickled cucumber. Add some pickled ginger and sprinkle with furikake seasoning to serve.

Broiled Mackerel with Orange Gremolata Dressing

Serves 4

4 mackerel fillets, skin on
Olive oil, for broiling
Juice of 1 small orange
4 rosemary sprigs, chopped in half

For the orange gremolata dressing
½ cup olive oil
2 garlic cloves, peeled and finely
  chopped
Zest and juice of 1 small orange
2 tablespoons roughly chopped flat-leaf
  parsley
Sea salt and freshly ground black
  pepper

Time-saving tip
Slash the skin of the mackerel
several times, as this allows the
heat to penetrate to the center
of the fish and speeds up the
cooking.

We spend a lot of time as a family in Cornwall, where the fish is amazing. In fact, we barbecue fresh mackerel throughout the summer, and this orange gremolata is one of our favorite accompaniments. It's quick to put together and packs a citrus punch that goes really well with the oily fish.

1 Preheat the broiler to medium-high. Line the broiler pan with foil.

2 To make the orange gremolata dressing, put all the ingredients for it into a bowl and season with salt and pepper. Mix well, then set aside.

3 Using a sharp knife, score the skin on the mackerel fillets, then place them on the prepared broiler pan, skin side down. Drizzle olive oil over each of the fillets, add a squeeze of orange juice, and scatter the rosemary sprigs on top.

4 Place the pan under the broiler and cook the fish for 1–2 minutes before turning over and cooking for another 4–5 minutes, until the skin is crisp and the flesh is opaque.

5 Transfer the fish to a platter and spoon over the gremolata dressing, before serving with a large green salad and lots of warm crusty bread.

Malaysian Fish and Okra Curry

Serves 4

2 tablespoons vegetable oil

1 onion, peeled and finely diced

3 garlic cloves, peeled and finely chopped

1-inch piece of fresh ginger, peeled and finely grated

1 long red chile, seeded if you want a milder hit, finely chopped

1 teaspoon Thai shrimp paste

1 heaping teaspoon ground turmeric

2 tomatoes, roughly chopped

1 cup fish stock

1⅔ cups coconut cream

1 makrut lime leaf

2 teaspoons lemongrass paste

1 teaspoon coconut palm sugar

1 tablespoon tamarind paste

1½ pounds monkfish fillets

7 ounces okra

2 tablespoons chopped cilantro

When you are tempted to order takeout, remember that this knockout Malaysian fish curry can be ready in just 30 minutes. It will be on the table before the delivery driver even sets off to your house! And this light but creamy, sweet-and-sour curry will blow most takeouts out of the water. I know that okra is a bit of a divisive vegetable, so leave it out if you don't like it.

1 Place a large nonstick sauté pan over medium-high heat and add the oil. When hot, add the onion and cook for 2–3 minutes, until softened.

2 Add the garlic, ginger, and chile and cook for 2 minutes before adding the shrimp paste and turmeric. Stir for 1 minute, or until fragrant, then add the tomatoes, fish stock, coconut cream, lime leaf, lemongrass paste, palm sugar, and tamarind paste. Stir well, bring to a boil, and simmer for 10–12 minutes.

3 Meanwhile, cut the monkfish into 1- to 2-inch pieces. Trim the okra and cut each one in half at an angle.

4 Add the okra to the pan and cook for 2 minutes, then add the monkfish and cook for an additional 5–6 minutes, until cooked through. Remove the pan from the heat, stir in the cilantro, and serve in bowls with basmati rice or Aromatic Saffron Pilaf (see page 204).

Tuna Steaks with Preserved Lemon Couscous

Serves 2

2 (7-ounce) tuna steaks
1 tablespoon olive oil

For the preserved lemon couscous
½ cup couscous
Pinch of saffron
½ preserved lemon, finely chopped
½ cup vegetable stock
¼ cucumber
2 tablespoons cilantro leaves
2 tablespoons mint leaves
1 (15-ounce) can of chickpeas, drained
   and rinsed
2 tablespoons extra virgin olive oil
Lemon juice, to taste
Sea salt and freshly ground black
   pepper

To serve
½ teaspoon sumac
Lemon wedges

If you have more time…
…make the Moroccan Carrot
Salad on page 199 to go with
this. It will turn a simple lunch
into a feast.

All types of fish are quick to cook, but tuna wins the speed prize because it's served rare in the middle and is literally in and out of the pan in 4 minutes. These steaks are seasoned with sumac, which has a lemony tang. It offsets the meaty tuna brilliantly and complements the Moroccan flavors in the couscous.

1 Put the couscous into a heatproof bowl. Using a mortar and pestle, grind the saffron to a powder, then place in a small saucepan with the preserved lemon and vegetable stock. Bring to a boil and pour over the couscous. Stir well, cover the bowl with plastic wrap, and leave to sit for 5–10 minutes.

2 Meanwhile, finely dice the cucumber and roughly chop the herbs.

3 Uncover the couscous and fluff it up with a fork. Add the cucumber, herbs, chickpeas, extra virgin olive oil, and a little lemon juice. Mix well and season with salt and pepper. Set aside.

4 Place a large nonstick frying pan over medium-high heat. Drizzle the tuna steaks with the olive oil and season both sides with salt and pepper. When the pan is smoking hot, add the tuna and cook for 2 minutes on each side.

5 Spoon the couscous onto plates and place the tuna on top. Sprinkle each plate with the sumac and serve with lemon wedges and a green salad.

Baked Halibut with Fennel, Carrot, and Lemon

Serves 2

1 large carrot
2 baby fennel bulbs
2 tablespoons olive oil
Zest and juice of 1 lemon
2 (5-ounce) halibut fillets
1 teaspoon fennel pollen (optional)
Sea salt and freshly ground
    black pepper

Time-saving tip

Using a mandoline or vegetable peeler to cut vegetables into ribbons means they will cook more quickly than if you slice them. You can also serve them raw for a crunchy salad.

I have seasoned these halibut fillets with fennel pollen, which is exactly what it sounds like—the pollen from fennel flowers, which has been sun-dried in southern Italy. I have made it optional, as it's an expensive ingredient, but you need only a little because it's so intense and a little goes a long way. Its anise flavor goes wonderfully with fish, chicken, and pork, and is also good lightly sprinkled over salads or couscous.

1   Preheat the oven to 400°F.
2   Cut two pieces of parchment paper about 13 x 16 inches, and fold each one in half lengthwise.
3   Peel the carrot and use a mandoline or vegetable peeler to slice into thin ribbons. Trim the fennel, reserving any fronds, and thinly slice the bulb into ribbons.
4   Divide the vegetables between the two pieces of parchment paper, placing them to the right of the fold. Pour over a tablespoon of oil, then sprinkle with any reserved fronds and the lemon zest.
5   Using a sharp knife, score the halibut skin, then place a fish fillet on top of the vegetables, skin side up, and season with salt and pepper. Squeeze the lemon juice over each fillet, then sprinkle with the fennel pollen (if using).
6   Fold the parchment paper over the fish and seal the long edges together by folding them over each other. Twist the ends and tuck them underneath. Put the parcels on a baking sheet and place on the top shelf of the oven for 8–10 minutes, until the fish is cooked through.
7   Serve the halibut in the paper bags with new potatoes and a green salad.

Garlic and Chile Shrimp

Serves 2

¼ cup olive oil
6 garlic cloves, peeled and finely
   chopped
1 red chile, seeded if you want
   a milder hit, finely chopped
Pinch of chile flakes (optional)
1½ pounds raw tiger shrimp (or other
   jumbo head-on shrimp)
⅓ cup Manzanilla sherry
1 teaspoon tomato purée
7 ounces cherry tomatoes, quartered
2 tablespoons butter, cut into ½-inch
   cubes
2 tablespoons chopped flat-leaf parsley
Sea salt and freshly ground black
   pepper

Shrimp—in fact, shellfish in general—are the perfect fast food because they take just a few minutes to cook. All the work here is in chopping the garlic and chile and quartering the tomatoes. Make sure you serve these lip-smackingly good shrimp with plenty of good bread for mopping up all the juices, and a lot of paper napkins, as things could get messy...

1 Place a large nonstick frying pan over medium-high heat and add the oil. When hot, add the garlic, chile, and chile flakes (if using), and stir gently for 1 minute.

2 Add the shrimp and cook until pink on one side. Turn each of the shrimp over and add the sherry, tomato purée, and cherry tomatoes. Cook for 1–2 minutes, until the shrimp are pink all over, then transfer the shrimp to a plate. Continue to cook the mixture in the pan for 2–3 more minutes, until the tomatoes have softened.

3 Return the shrimp to the pan, stir in the butter and parsley, and season to taste. Serve with a green salad and some crusty bread to mop up the delicious sauce.

Pan-Seared Salmon with Warm Potato Salad

Serves 4

1½ pounds new potatoes
½ teaspoon salt
1 bay leaf
2 thyme sprigs
5 black peppercorns
2 shallots
2 tablespoons chopped dill
1 tablespoon olive oil
4 salmon fillets, skin on
½ cup crème fraîche
2 tablespoons nonpareil capers
Sea salt and freshly ground black
    pepper
Lemon wedges, to serve

This dish might seem a little old-fashioned, but I don't think you can beat a simple, unadorned piece of salmon with warm potatoes dressed Scandinavian style with crème fraîche, capers, and dill. Make sure you choose the freshest, most ethically sourced salmon possible, and don't overcook it—the skin should be crisp but the flesh should still be a little translucent in the middle.

1   Bring a kettle of water to a boil, then pour it into a saucepan. Add the potatoes, salt, bay leaf, thyme sprigs, and peppercorns, cover the pan with a lid, and bring to a boil. Once boiling, remove the lid, reduce the heat, and simmer for 10–12 minutes, until cooked through.

2   While the potatoes are cooking, peel and finely chop the shallots.

3   Once the potatoes are cooked, drain and lay them out on a cutting board to cool a little. Discard the bay leaf, thyme twigs, and peppercorns.

4   Place a large frying pan over medium-high heat and add the olive oil. Season the salmon fillets with salt and, once the oil is hot, add them to the pan, skin side down. Cook for 3–4 minutes before turning over and cooking for another 1–2 minutes. Remove the pan from the heat and set aside.

5   Using a clean dish towel to protect your hand, slice the hot potatoes and put them into a bowl with the shallots, dill, crème fraîche, and capers. Stir to combine, and season generously with salt and black pepper.

6   Place the salmon fillets on plates with a lemon wedge alongside, and add a generous spoonful of the warm potatoes. Serve with a green salad.

Chinese-Style Baked Sea Bass

Serves 2

4 baby bok choy, cut in half lengthwise

5 ounces green beans, trimmed

3 ounces baby corn, larger ones halved
lengthwise

2 (6-ounce) sea bass fillets, skin on

2-inch piece of fresh ginger, peeled and
julienned

2 garlic cloves, peeled and thinly sliced

1 long red chile, seeded if you want a
milder hit, thinly sliced

½ teaspoon cornstarch

2 tablespoons soy sauce

1 tablespoon oyster sauce

1 tablespoon sesame oil, plus extra to
serve

¼ cup Shaoxing rice wine

Pinch of ground white pepper

Jasmine rice, to serve

Cooking fish in a bag (en papillote) is a great way to impart flavor into the flesh, and there is the added bonus of very little mess to wash up afterward. Here I have seasoned the sea bass with ginger, chile, and garlic as well as rice wine, sesame oil, and oyster sauce, so the aroma that hits you when you open the bag is sensational.

1 Preheat the oven to 425°F.

2 Cut two pieces of parchment paper about 14 x 16 inches, and fold each one in half lengthwise. Lay the bok choy to the right of each fold. Put the beans on top, then place the corn on top of the beans.

3 Cut each sea bass fillet in half across the middle and place two halves, overlapping slightly, on top of the vegetables.

4 Sprinkle the ginger, garlic, and chile over the fish.

5 Put the cornstarch in a bowl with the soy sauce and mix until well combined. Add the oyster sauce, sesame oil, rice wine, and white pepper and mix again. Spoon the mixture over the fish.

6 Fold the parchment paper over the fish and seal the edges together by folding them over each other. Twist the ends and tuck them underneath. Put the parcels on a baking sheet and place on the top shelf of the oven for 15 minutes.

7 Place the parcels on two serving plates, open them up, and drizzle with a little extra sesame oil before serving with jasmine rice.

Salt and Pink Pepper Shrimp with Lime Mayonnaise

Serves 4

1 tablespoon pink peppercorns
½ teaspoon sea salt
Zest and juice of 2 limes
3 tablespoons olive oil
1 pound raw, peeled tail-on jumbo shrimp
1 tablespoon roughly chopped cilantro

For the lime mayonnaise
½ cup mayonnaise
Juice of 1 lime

Pink peppercorns aren't technically peppercorns at all; they're actually a type of berry, but they have a peppery taste and aroma, and, although a bit milder, can be used in many of the same dishes as regular pepper. Here the combination of pink pepper, lime, and cilantro marries beautifully with the sweetness of the shrimp for a cracking starter or main course.

1 Using a mortar and pestle, grind the peppercorns and salt into a coarse powder.

2 Put the lime zest and juice into a large bowl, then stir in the olive oil and pink pepper mixture.

3 Add the shrimp and, using clean hands, toss gently until they are well coated.

4 Mix the mayonnaise and lime juice together in a small bowl.

5 Place a large nonstick frying pan over medium-high heat and, when very hot, add the shrimp. Cook for 2–3 minutes, stirring regularly, until all the shrimp are pink and cooked through.

6 Tip the shrimp onto a platter, sprinkle with the cilantro, and serve immediately with the lime mayonnaise and a big green salad.

Roast Hake with Saffron Mayonnaise

Serves 4

10 ounces Broccolini

4 (7-ounce) hake fillets, skinned and
pinboned

1 tablespoon thyme leaves

2 tablespoons extra virgin olive oil

Zest and juice of ½ orange

1 lemon, cut into wedges

For the saffron mayonnaise

Pinch of saffron

1 tablespoon boiling water

2 egg yolks

2 small garlic cloves, peeled and
crushed

1 tablespoon Dijon mustard

⅓ cup olive oil

⅓ cup vegetable oil

Lemon juice, to taste

Sea salt and freshly ground black
pepper

Chef's tip

Grinding your saffron threads
in a mortar and pouring over a
little hot water before using will
get the maximum flavor out
of this expensive spice.

**Hake is a meaty whitefish with a mild flavor that is
increasingly replacing less-sustainable haddock and
cod on menus. I love it for its slightly sweet-tasting
flesh and its ability to take on other flavors as diverse
as chorizo and, as here, orange and saffron. I know it's
easier to open a jar of mayo than to make your own,
but the flavor of homemade is incomparable, so give
this a go.**

1   Preheat the oven to 400°F.

2   Using a mortar and pestle, grind the saffron to a
powder, then add the boiling water and leave to sit.

3   Put the Broccolini into a large roasting pan and place
the hake fillets on top, skin side down. Sprinkle with
the thyme, salt, and pepper, then drizzle with the olive
oil. Add a little orange zest to each piece of hake.

4   Place the pan in the oven on a high shelf for 10–15
minutes, until the fish is cooked through and the
Broccolini is slightly charred.

5   Meanwhile, make the mayonnaise. Put the egg yolks,
garlic, and mustard into a bowl. Whisk well, then pour
the two oils into the bowl in a gentle stream while
whisking constantly. Add the saffron water and a little
salt and pepper and whisk again. Add lemon juice
to taste.

6   Remove the hake from oven and squeeze over the
orange juice. Leave to rest for 2–3 minutes, then serve
with a big dollop of the saffron mayonnaise and a lemon
wedge on each plate.

Poultry

Saffron Chicken Flatbreads with Minted Yogurt

Serves 2

Pinch of saffron
1 tablespoon boiling water
1 pound boneless, skinless chicken
   thighs
2 garlic cloves, peeled and crushed
1 teaspoon thyme leaves
Zest of 1 lemon
¼ cup Greek yogurt
1 red onion, peeled and cut into
   8 wedges
2 flatbreads
2 large handfuls of mixed salad greens
5 ounces cherry tomatoes, halved
2 tablespoons crispy fried onions
   (available from supermarkets), to
   serve (optional)

For the minted yogurt
¾ cup Greek yogurt
Small handful of mint leaves, finely
   chopped
Lemon juice, to taste

> ### Chef's tip
> Whenever using wooden skewers
> for broiling or barbecuing, you will
> need to soak them in water for
> at least 30 minutes in advance
> of cooking or they will burn.

When we're in LA, we like to barbecue almost all year round, and chicken on sticks is a family favorite, probably because it's so easy and there are endless variations. I love using the mild-mannered spice saffron, which stains the meat golden yellow and imparts a gentle Mediterranean scent to everything. The fresh minted yogurt is the perfect accompaniment, but you could replace it with tzatziki if you're in a rush.

1 Soak 4 bamboo skewers in water for at least 30 minutes. Preheat the oven to 450°F.
2 Using a mortar and pestle, grind the saffron to a powder, then cover with the boiling water and leave to sit.
3 Cut the chicken into 2-inch pieces and place in a bowl with the garlic, thyme, lemon zest, and yogurt. Season with salt and pepper, add the saffron water, and mix well.
4 Thread the chicken pieces onto the skewers, alternating them with the red onion. Place on a nonstick roasting pan and put on a high shelf in the oven for 12 minutes.
5 Meanwhile, make the minted yogurt. Combine the yogurt with the mint, add lemon juice to taste, and season with a little salt and pepper. Set aside until needed.
6 Put the flatbreads on a baking sheet and place in the bottom of the oven to warm for a few minutes.
7 Preheat the broiler. When the chicken has been cooking for 12 minutes, place it under the broiler and cook for an additional 3–4 minutes, until golden brown and cooked through.
8 Put the flatbreads on plates and spread some of the minted yogurt down the middle. Add a handful of the salad greens to each and divide the tomatoes between them. Put the cooked skewers on top and sprinkle with fried onions to serve.

Asian Duck Salad

Serves 2

2 duck breasts
1 teaspoon Chinese five-spice powder
6 radishes, thinly sliced
⅓ cucumber, halved lengthwise
  and sliced at an angle
2 large handfuls of watercress
2 large handfuls of bean sprouts
2 large handfuls of mixed salad greens
Small handful of cilantro leaves
1 teaspoon toasted sesame seeds
1 long red chile, seeded if you want a
  milder hit, thinly sliced at an angle
2 spring onions, green parts only, thinly
  sliced lengthwise
Sea salt and freshly ground black
  pepper

For the dressing
1½ tablespoons hoisin sauce
1 teaspoon peeled and grated fresh
  ginger
1 tablespoon sesame oil
1 tablespoon rice vinegar
Juice of ½ lime

Time-saving tip
When you are grating ingredients, such as ginger, lime zest, or cheese, grate onto a plate rather than a cutting board. It's much quicker and easier to tip the ingredient into the pan, and you don't leave half of it behind on the board.

Duck is quite a dense meat, but because it's served pink in the middle, it's relatively quick to cook. The robust, gamy flavor of the duck goes brilliantly with Chinese five-spice, which is a mix of star anise, Chinese cinnamon, Sichuan pepper, cloves, and fennel seed. It gives an instant Asian vibe to stir-fries, ribs, chicken wings, and pork, or use it in baking to add a new dimension to cakes and fruit desserts.

1 Preheat the oven to 400°F.
2 Using a very sharp knife, score the skin on the duck breasts in diagonal lines, first in one direction, then the other so you have a diamond pattern. Rub in the Chinese five-spice, then season both sides with salt and pepper.
3 Put the duck breasts, skin side down, in a nonstick, ovenproof frying pan. Place the pan over medium-high heat and cook for 7 minutes, or until the fat has rendered and the skin is crisp and golden.
4 Meanwhile, put the radishes and cucumber into a salad bowl with the watercress, bean sprouts, mixed salad greens, and cilantro.
5 Make the dressing by whisking all the ingredients together.
6 Turn the duck breasts over and place the frying pan in the oven for 3–4 minutes. Remove from the oven and leave to rest for 2–3 minutes.
7 Add half the dressing to the salad bowl and mix well. Divide the salad between two serving plates.
8 Carve the duck into thick slices and arrange on top of the salad. Spoon over the remaining dressing and sprinkle with the sesame seeds, chile, and spring onions before serving.

Moroccan Chicken and Couscous

Serves 4

7 ounces baby carrots

2 red onions, peeled and each
cut into 8 wedges

2 tablespoons olive oil

2 tablespoons ras-el-hanout

1 cup chicken stock

1 cup couscous

4 chicken breasts, skin on

2 zucchinis

1 (14-ounce) can of chickpeas,
drained and rinsed

¼ cup water

¼ cup chopped cilantro

Lemon juice, to taste

2 tablespoons sliced pistachios,
roughly chopped

Sea salt and freshly ground black
pepper

Rose petals, to serve (optional)

Using a spice mix like ras-el-hanout is a great kitchen shortcut—just sprinkle it over the vegetables and chicken in this easy dish and you will be instantly transported to the souks of Morocco or Tunis without any effort at all. However, keep an eye on the sell-by date of ground spices—after a year or two they lose their potency, so don't let them languish in the back of your pantry for more than a decade and then expect them to taste of anything.

1   Preheat the oven to 425°F.

2   Wash the baby carrots, cutting any larger ones in half lengthwise. Place in a large roasting pan with the onions. Drizzle with 1 tablespoon of the olive oil and sprinkle over 1 tablespoon of the ras-el-hanout until evenly coated. Place in the oven for 10 minutes.

3   Pour the chicken stock into a small pan, place over medium-high heat, and bring to a boil. Put the couscous into a bowl with a little salt and pepper. Pour the hot stock over it, cover with plastic wrap, and set aside to absorb the liquid.

4   Score the chicken skin with a sharp knife, then season with salt and pepper and sprinkle over ½ tablespoon of the remaining ras-el-hanout.

5   Cut each zucchini into quarters lengthwise and then into 2-inch lengths, then sprinkle with the remaining ½ tablespoon ras-el-hanout. Remove the pan from the oven and add the zucchini and chickpeas. Place the chicken breasts on top and drizzle with the remaining 1 tablespoon of olive oil. Add the water to the bottom of the pan and return to the oven on a high shelf for 15 minutes.

6   Meanwhile, uncover the couscous and fluff it up with a fork. Stir in the cilantro, then add lemon juice and salt and pepper to taste.

7   Remove the roasting pan from the oven and sprinkle with pistachios and rose petals (if using). Bring to the table and serve straight from the pan.

Buffalo Chicken and Blue Cheese Dressing

Serves 2

8 chicken tenders
1¼ cups buttermilk
1½ teaspoons garlic granules
1½ teaspoons onion powder
1 teaspoon dried thyme
½ teaspoon cayenne pepper
Vegetable oil, for frying
1¼ cups all-purpose flour
⅓ cup Frank's RedHot Wings Sauce
Sea salt and freshly ground
    black pepper

For the dressing
¼ cup Greek yogurt
¼ cup sour cream
1 tablespoon mayonnaise
1 ounce blue cheese, crumbled
Squeeze of lemon juice
2 dashes of Worcestershire sauce

To serve
Celery sticks
Little Gem lettuce leaves

If you have more time...
...leave the chicken tenders in the buttermilk marinade overnight; they will be even more tender when it comes to cooking them.

As I spend a lot of time in the United States these days and have eight restaurants there now, I have become partial to some of the classic foods of America. This is my take on buffalo chicken with blue cheese dip and hot sauce, and it is finger-licking good, if I say so myself. Using chicken tenders keeps the cooking time short, and they are easy to pick up and eat without getting yourself into a sticky mess.

1 Preheat the oven to 250°F.
2 Put the chicken into a bowl with the buttermilk, garlic granules, onion powder, thyme, cayenne pepper, and a little salt and pepper. Mix well.
3 Heat a one-third depth of oil in a large pan to 375°F, or until a cube of bread browns in 25 seconds.
4 Meanwhile, mix all the dressing ingredients together. Season to taste.
5 Put the flour into a shallow bowl, add some salt and pepper, and mix well. Take a tender out of the marinade, keeping as much buttermilk on it as possible, and coat in the flour. Transfer to a plate while you repeat this step with 3 more tenders.
6 Once the oil has reached temperature, carefully add the coated tenders and cook for 4–5 minutes, until deep golden brown and cooked through. Drain on paper towels, then transfer to a baking sheet and place in the oven to keep warm.
7 Flour the remaining chicken tenders while you bring the oil back up to temperature. When it's hot enough, carefully add the tenders and cook for 4–5 minutes. Drain on paper towels, then keep warm with the other tenders.
8 Pour the RedHot Wings Sauce and blue cheese dressing into serving bowls, and serve alongside the chicken with celery sticks and lettuce.

Wild Leek Turkey Kievs

Serves 2

7 tablespoons butter, softened
2 tablespoons roughly chopped
   tarragon
Zest of ½ lemon
2 small garlic cloves, peeled and
   crushed
Large handful of wild leeks, roughly
   chopped
1 egg
⅓ cup all-purpose flour
¼ cup milk
⅔ cup panko breadcrumbs
1 tablespoon finely chopped flat-leaf
   parsley or dill
4 (3½-ounce) turkey cutlets
5 ounces green beans, trimmed
Vegetable oil, for frying
Sea salt and freshly ground black
   pepper

It's back to the 1970s with this retro dish, but these days I use turkey (the breasts are so much bigger and easier to work with) and wild leeks for a more subtle, sophisticated flavor. If it isn't wild leek season and you haven't got any wild leek in the freezer (see Chef's tip, page 41), add another regular garlic clove to the recipe.

1 Put the butter, tarragon, lemon zest, garlic, and wild leeks into a small food processor. Season with a little salt and pepper and blend until well combined.

2 Put the egg, flour, and milk in a shallow bowl and whisk together to make a batter.

3 Mix the panko breadcrumbs with the parsley in a second shallow bowl.

4 Lay 2 of the cutlets on a piece of plastic wrap so that they are slightly overlapping. Bash them lightly with a rolling pin to join them together and to make the meat an even thickness.

5 Put half the wild leek butter on one half of the joined cutlet, leaving a ½-inch border around it. Spread a little batter all the way around the edges, then fold the cutlet over the wild leek butter and press down to seal well. Repeat steps 4 and 5 with the remaining cutlets.

6 Dip each Kiev in the batter, making sure they are coated evenly, then cover in the panko breadcrumbs. Place them in the fridge for 5 minutes.

7 Meanwhile, cook the green beans in salted boiling water until tender. Drain and keep warm until needed.

8 Place a sauté pan over medium-high heat and add a 1-inch depth of oil. When hot (340–350°F), carefully place each Kiev in the oil and cook for 3–4 minutes on each side, until deep golden and cooked through. Drain on paper towels and serve immediately with the green beans.

Chinese-Style Ginger Chicken with Garlic Rice

Serves 4

4 chicken breasts, skin on
1½-inch piece of fresh ginger,
    peeled and julienned
6 spring onions—4 trimmed
    and cut in half; 2 green part
    only, thinly sliced, to serve
2 cups chicken stock
2 tablespoons Shaoxing rice wine
1 tablespoon light soy sauce
Sea salt

For the garlic rice
1½ cups jasmine rice
1 tablespoon vegetable oil
1 tablespoon sesame oil
3 large garlic cloves, peeled
    and finely chopped
2 cups chicken stock
Pinch of ground white pepper

For many people, chicken is the mainstay of the midweek supper, and I think some of us are always on the lookout for new and interesting ways of serving it. This recipe is quick, full of flavor, and bound to be popular. Crisping the skin as described is a really easy trick for adding crunch and flavor. It's not an essential step, but it will take this dish to the next level.

1 Preheat the oven to 400°F.
2 Remove the skin from the chicken breasts and scrape any excess fat off it with a sharp knife. Season both sides of the skin with salt and place on a baking sheet. Place another baking sheet on top to keep the skin flat and place in the oven for 12–15 minutes, until golden and crisp. Set aside to cool.
3 Put the chicken breasts, ginger, spring onion halves, and 2 cups chicken stock into a saucepan, place over high heat, and bring to a boil.
4 Meanwhile, wash the jasmine rice three times and drain thoroughly. Heat the vegetable oil and sesame oil in a saucepan, then add the garlic and cook for 2 minutes. Add the rice, 2 cups chicken stock, and the pepper and bring to a boil. Place a lid on the pan, reduce the heat to low, and simmer for 5–8 minutes, until the rice is cooked.
5 Once the chicken pan is boiling, reduce the heat and simmer gently for 5 minutes. Remove the chicken from the pan and set aside to rest. Discard the spring onions, then rapidly return the stock to a boil. Add the Shaoxing wine and soy sauce and cook for another 5 minutes.
6 Spoon the rice into bowls, then slice the chicken and lay it on top. Ladle the stock over and garnish with the spring onion greens. Crumble a piece of chicken skin over each bowl to serve.

Crispy Chicken Thighs with Romesco Sauce

Serves 2

4 chicken thighs, bone in and skin on
2 tablespoons olive oil
3½ ounces lacinato kale
1 tablespoon water
4 ounces Padrón or shishito peppers
Sea salt and freshly ground black
  pepper

For the sauce

5 ounces roasted peppers, from a jar
1 garlic clove, peeled and crushed
3 tablespoons toasted blanched
  almonds
1 tablespoon sherry vinegar
¼ teaspoon sweet smoked paprika
1 slice sourdough bread, crust
  removed
3 tablespoons extra virgin olive oil

Romesco is a vibrant red pepper sauce given texture by blitzed almonds. It's a dream with chicken, but it can also be served with fish, shrimp, and roasted leeks. Brilliantly, you can buy roasted red peppers in a jar, so you don't have to prepare them yourself, making this sauce almost completely hassle-free.

1 Preheat the oven to 400°F.
2 Season the chicken thighs with salt and pepper. Place a large ovenproof frying pan over high heat. When hot, add 1 tablespoon of the olive oil and put the chicken thighs in skin side down. Reduce the heat to medium and cook the chicken for 8 minutes.
3 Once the chicken skin is golden brown and crisp, turn the thighs over and add the kale and water. Season with a little salt and pepper, then place the whole pan in the oven for 8 minutes.
4 Meanwhile, place all the romesco sauce ingredients in a small food processor with a little salt and pepper and blend until smooth.
5 Place a small frying pan over high heat. When very hot, add the remaining 1 tablespoon of olive oil, the Padrón peppers, and a sprinkle of salt. Cook for 4–5 minutes, until the skin on the peppers has blistered and softened.
6 Remove the chicken from the pan and set aside to rest. Mix the kale into the pan juices and serve with the chicken, Padrón peppers, and a generous spoonful of the romesco sauce.

Double Lemon Chicken

Serves 4

2 tablespoons olive oil

8 chicken thighs, bone in and skin on

5 garlic cloves, peeled and crushed
with the blade of a chef's knife

3 thyme sprigs

1 fresh lemon

1 preserved lemon

1 tablespoon sherry vinegar

2 tablespoons dark soy sauce

3½ tablespoons runny honey

1 tablespoon water

2 tablespoons roughly chopped
flat-leaf parsley

Sea salt and freshly ground black
pepper

Chef's tip

To get more juice out of a lemon,
heat it in the microwave for
20 seconds on full power before
squeezing it. The heat helps break
down the membranes in the fruit,
which means the juice is released
more easily.

Lemon and chicken is a classic pairing, but by adding both fresh and preserved lemons to this recipe, the lemon flavor is intensified and it becomes something new. The almost molten sauce is sweet, sticky, and utterly delicious. Serve with mashed potatoes (see page 207), lightly cooked green vegetables, or a simple salad to counterbalance the richness.

1 Preheat the oven to 400°F.

2 Place a large ovenproof frying pan over high heat and, when hot, add the olive oil. Season the chicken thighs with salt and pepper and add them to the pan with the garlic and thyme sprigs. Cook for 2–3 minutes on each side, until golden brown.

3 Meanwhile, slice the fresh lemon very thinly on a mandoline, and roughly chop the preserved lemon.

4 Add the sherry vinegar to the frying pan and allow to reduce by half before adding the soy sauce and honey. Shake the pan to mix the sauce and reduce the heat to medium-high.

5 Pour in the 1 tablespoon of water, then add the fresh and preserved lemons and bring to a simmer. Place in the oven for 10–15 minutes, until the chicken is cooked through and the sauce has reduced to a thick syrup.

6 Transfer the chicken to a serving dish and sprinkle with the parsley before serving with green vegetables or a salad.

Thai Chile and Basil Chicken

Serves 4

2 cups jasmine rice

2¾ cups water

3 skinless, boneless chicken breasts, thinly sliced

About ¼ cup vegetable oil

2 tablespoons oyster sauce

1 tablespoon soy sauce

⅓ cup chicken stock

2 tablespoons fish sauce

1 tablespoon superfine sugar

1 tablespoon cornstarch

1 tablespoon water

5 garlic cloves, peeled and finely chopped

4 Thai bird's-eye chiles, thinly sliced

1 onion, peeled and thickly sliced

5 ounces Broccolini, cut into 2-inch lengths

5 ounces green beans, trimmed and halved

Large handful of Thai basil leaves

Small handful of Italian basil leaves

Sea salt and ground white pepper

Thai basil is woodier and more robust than Italian basil, and has a spicy anise flavor that is quite distinct from its European cousin's. It isn't always easy to get hold of, but it's worth trying to track down to experience for yourself. When stir-frying, efficiency is everything—get all your ingredients prepped before you start and the process of getting dinner on the table will be seamless.

1 Wash the rice three times until the water runs clear, then place in a saucepan with the measured water and a pinch of salt. Bring to a boil, then reduce the heat to a low simmer and place a lid on the pan. Cook for an additional 10–12 minutes, until the liquid has gone and the rice is cooked.

2 Meanwhile, prepare the meat and all the vegetables for the stir-fry. Season the chicken with salt and white pepper.

3 Place a wok over very high heat until smoking hot. Add 1 tablespoon vegetable oil and stir-fry a quarter of the chicken for 1 minute, or until it has browned lightly. Quickly remove the wok from the heat and transfer the chicken to a plate. Return the wok to the heat and cook the remaining chicken in the same way, adding more oil as necessary.

4 Combine the oyster sauce, soy sauce, chicken stock, fish sauce, and sugar in a small bowl. In a separate bowl, mix the cornstarch with the water.

5 Put the wok back on the heat, adding more oil as necessary, then stir-fry the garlic and half the chiles for 1 minute.

6 Add the onion and stir-fry for 2 minutes. Add the Broccolini and green beans and cook for 2 minutes, adding a little water if they begin to stick.

7 Return the chicken to the wok and cook for an additional 2–3 minutes.

8 Add the oyster and soy sauce mixture to the wok, and then stir in the cornstarch paste and Thai basil leaves and cook for 1 more minute.

9 Spoon the rice and stir-fry into bowls and sprinkle with the remaining chiles and Italian basil leaves before serving.

Chicken Ramen

Serves 2

2 eggs

2 tablespoons vegetable oil

2 chicken breasts, skin on

3½ ounces ramen noodles

2 large handfuls of baby spinach

2 large handfuls of bean sprouts

1 quart chicken stock

1 tablespoon white miso paste

2 teaspoons dashi powder

2 tablespoons soy sauce

3 garlic cloves, peeled and thinly sliced

1½-inch piece of fresh ginger, peeled and julienned

2 tablespoons saké (Japanese rice wine)

1 long red chile, seeded if you want a milder hit, thinly sliced at an angle

2 spring onions, trimmed and thinly sliced at an angle

1 teaspoon furikake seasoning

Sea salt and ground white pepper

Sesame oil, to serve

Originally an import from China, the Japanese have made this noodle soup their own by flavoring the broth with ingredients such as miso, kombu, and katsuobushi (dried tuna flakes). I use miso and dashi powder to give it that authentic taste, both of which are available from Asian supermarkets or online. In Japan, it isn't rude to slurp as you eat the noodles or to put the bowl to your lips to drink the last bit of the soup, so feel free!

1 Bring a kettle of water to a boil, pour into a saucepan, and bring back to a boil over high heat. Gently lower the eggs into it and cook for 5–6 minutes for a slightly runny yolk.

2 Meanwhile, put the vegetable oil in a nonstick frying pan and place over high heat. Season the chicken breasts with salt and a little white pepper and place in the pan, skin side down. Cook over medium heat for 4–5 minutes on one side.

3 Using a slotted spoon, transfer the eggs to a bowl of cold water to stop them from cooking.

4 Add some salt to the water in the saucepan and bring back to a boil. Add the noodles and cook for 3–4 minutes, until just tender. Drain and divide between two serving bowls. Add a handful of baby spinach and a handful of bean sprouts to each bowl.

5 Carefully peel the eggs and cut them in half lengthwise.

6 Pour the chicken stock into a saucepan, add the miso paste, dashi powder, and soy sauce, then place the pan over medium heat.

7 Turn the chicken breasts over and add the garlic and ginger to the pan. Cook for another 2–3 minutes, stirring the garlic and ginger often. Add the saké and cook for another 2 minutes.

8 When the chicken is cooked, remove it from the pan to rest. Add the pan juices, along with the garlic and ginger, to the chicken stock and stir well.

9 Slice the chicken and place on top of the noodles. Ladle over the stock and garnish with the chile, spring onions, and furikake seasoning. Add the halved eggs to the bowls, drizzle with a little sesame oil, and serve.

Pan-Seared Duck Breast with Bok Choy and Orange Sauce

Serves 4

4 duck breasts
4 heads baby bok choy, halved
1 cup orange juice
¼ cup soy sauce
¾-inch piece of fresh ginger, peeled and grated
3½ tablespoons butter
2½ tablespoons runny honey
1 tablespoon black and white sesame seeds
Sea salt and freshly ground black pepper
Cooked rice, to serve

Chef's tip
Before measuring honey, coat the measuring spoon or bowl with a thin layer of flavorless cooking oil, and the honey will slip straight off into the pan or mixing bowl without leaving a sticky mess behind. It's more accurate too.

Duck with orange is clearly a tried-and-tested combination, but adding soy sauce, honey, and ginger gives it an Asian twist that freshens up the old French classic. Make sure you get quite a bit of color on the bok choy before adding the sauce ingredients— the bitterness of the charred edges offsets the sweetness beautifully.

1 Preheat the oven to 400°F and place a baking sheet inside to heat up.

2 Using a very sharp knife, score the skin on the duck breasts in diagonal lines, first in one direction, then the other so you have a diamond pattern. Season well with salt and pepper.

3 Put the duck breasts, skin side down, in a nonstick, ovenproof frying pan. Place the pan over medium-high heat and cook for 7 minutes, or until the fat has rendered and the skin is crisp and golden.

4 Turn the duck breasts over and place the frying pan in the oven for 3–4 minutes. Transfer the duck to a warm plate and leave to rest for 2–3 minutes.

5 Meanwhile, return the frying pan to the stovetop and add the halved bok choy. Cook for 2 minutes, or until beginning to color, then add the orange juice, soy sauce, ginger, and butter and bring to a simmer. Stir in the honey and reduce to a thick sauce.

6 To serve, slice the duck at an angle and plate up with the bok choy and some cooked rice. Pour over the sauce and sprinkle with the sesame seeds before serving.

Pancetta-Wrapped Chicken with Glazed Carrots and Mustard Sauce

Serves 2

12 thin slices of pancetta
2 boneless, skinless chicken breasts
Sea salt and freshly ground black
    pepper
1 tablespoon mild olive oil
1 shallot, peeled and finely chopped
1 teaspoon grainy mustard
1 teaspoon Dijon mustard
1 teaspoon thyme leaves
¼ cup dry white wine
⅔ cup chicken stock
½ cup heavy cream

For the glazed carrots

10 ounces Chantenay or baby carrots
3 tablespoons butter
1 cup chicken stock
1 teaspoon honey
1 tablespoon finely chopped flat-leaf
    parsley
Sea salt and freshly ground black
    pepper

If you have more time...
...make the Garlic and Herb
Mash (see page 207); it would
go brilliantly with this richly
flavored dish.

Wrapping lean chicken breasts in pancetta stops them from drying out and adds a delicious salty crunch. Don't be tempted to cook the carrots in a saucepan— it is the wide surface area of the frying pan that allows the cooking liquor to reduce to a glaze.

1 Preheat the oven to 425°F.

2 Wash the carrots and put them into a large frying pan with the butter, chicken stock, and honey. Add a little salt and pepper and place over high heat. Bring to a boil, then reduce the heat to a strong simmer and cook for about 15 minutes, stirring occasionally, until the carrots are tender.

3 Meanwhile, lay 6 slices of pancetta on a cutting board, overlapping them slightly. Season the chicken breasts with salt and pepper and place one of them in the middle of the pancetta. Wrap the pancetta around it, then repeat this step with the second one.

4 Place a nonstick frying pan over high heat. When hot, add the oil, then the chicken breasts and cook for 2–3 minutes on each side, or until the pancetta is golden brown all over. Transfer to a small baking sheet and place in the oven for 5 minutes.

5 Return the frying pan to the heat, add the shallot, and cook for 2 minutes, or until softened. Stir in the mustards and thyme leaves, then add the wine and allow it to reduce by half over high heat. Add the stock and cream, season with a little salt and pepper, and reduce until the sauce thickens.

6 Remove the chicken from the oven, keep warm, and allow to rest for 10 minutes.

7 Check on the carrots—they should be cooked and the sauce should have reduced to a glaze. Stir in the parsley and remove the pan from the heat.

8 Serve the chicken breasts with the glazed carrots, spooning the sauce over the top or serving it in small side dishes.

Meat

Steak Tacos with Pink Pickled Onion and Pico de Gallo

Serves 2

2 (8-ounce) flank steaks
1 teaspoon ground cumin
1 teaspoon Mexican chili powder
2 tablespoons mild olive oil
6–8 (6-inch) round yellow or blue corn
   tortillas
Sea salt and freshly ground black
   pepper

For the pickled onion

2 red onions, peeled and thinly sliced
¼ teaspoon dried oregano
Juice of 1 lime

For the pico de gallo

7 ounces cherry tomatoes, quartered
1 jalapeño chile, seeded; if you want a
   milder hit, sliced
Small handful of cilantro, roughly
   chopped
1 ripe avocado, peeled, pitted and
   diced
Squeeze of lime juice

For the chipotle crema

½ cup sour cream
2 teaspoons chipotle paste

Mexican street food is everywhere in LA, and I love the many different variations of tacos you can buy—pork, beef, chicken, and fish in amazing sauces. The great thing about making tacos at home is that everyone can fill their own, leaving out the bits they don't like, and adding plenty of what they do like. Pico de gallo, a roughly chopped salsa, doesn't usually contain avocado, but I love the creaminess it adds.

1 Sprinkle the steaks with the cumin and chili powder. Drizzle with the olive oil and season with salt and pepper.

2 Put the sliced onions into a small bowl and cover with boiling water. Leave for 10 minutes.

3 Meanwhile, make the pico de gallo: put the tomatoes and jalapeño into a small bowl with the cilantro, avocado, and lime juice. Season to taste.

4 Drain the onions, then place them in a small bowl. Add the oregano, lime juice, and a little salt and stir to combine.

5 Heat a large nonstick frying pan over high heat and cook the steaks for 3–4 minutes on each side. Transfer to a warm plate and leave to rest.

6 Heat the tortillas in a large frying pan one at a time until lightly toasted on each side.

7 Make the chipotle crema by mixing the sour cream with the chipotle paste.

8 Carve the steaks into thick slices. Place the tortillas on two plates and spoon some crema over them. Top with slices of steak, some pico de gallo, and pink onions and serve straight away.

Pork Schnitzel with Celeriac Remoulade

Serves 2

2 (8-ounce) boneless pork chops
½ cup all-purpose flour
1 egg
¾ cup fresh breadcrumbs
1 teaspoon dried dill
1 teaspoon paprika
Vegetable oil, for frying
Sea salt and freshly ground black
   pepper

For the remoulade
7 ounces celeriac, peeled and
   julienned
2 tablespoons mayonnaise
1 teaspoon grainy mustard
2 tablespoons sour cream
1 tablespoon finely chopped flat-leaf
   parsley
Squeeze of lemon juice

To serve
2 small handfuls of watercress
Lemon wedges (optional)

Schnitzel is a real crowd pleaser in our house—I think it's the crunch of the breadcrumbs with the salty savoriness of the pork that appeals to kids and adults alike. It's quick too, as the chops are flattened before you cook them, reducing the time they spend in the pan. The remoulade is only super-fast if you have a food processor to shred the celeriac—doing it by hand will take much longer.

1   Using a sharp knife, trim the fat off each pork chop. Lay them between two pieces of plastic wrap and use a mallet or rolling pin to flatten them out to a thickness of ⅛ inch.

2   Put the flour into a shallow bowl, season with salt and pepper, and mix well. Lightly beat the egg in a second shallow bowl. Put the breadcrumbs into a third shallow bowl and mix in the dill and paprika. Season both sides of the chops, then coat each one first in the flour, then in the egg, and finally in the breadcrumbs.

3   For the remoulade, put the celeriac, mayonnaise, mustard, sour cream, and parsley into a large bowl and mix well. Add a little lemon juice and season to taste. Set aside.

4   Heat a ½-inch depth of vegetable oil in a frying pan. When hot (340–350°F), carefully add the schnitzels and cook for 2–3 minutes on each side. Drain on paper towels.

5   Serve the schnitzels with a generous spoonful of the remoulade, a handful of watercress, and a lemon wedge (if using) on the side.

Bacon Cheeseburgers with Pickled Cucumber Burger Sauce

Serves 4

4 extra thick slices of smoked back
    bacon
2 pounds 80% lean ground beef
1 tablespoon mild olive oil
4 slices of Monterey jack or Cheddar
    cheese
4 burger buns with sesame seeds
1–2 tomatoes, thickly sliced
Small handful of dill pickle chips
2 large handfuls of shredded iceberg
    lettuce
Sea salt and freshly ground black
    pepper

For the burger sauce

½ cup mayonnaise
2 teaspoons yellow mustard
1 tablespoon tomato ketchup
¼ cup pickled cucumber relish
1 tablespoon white wine vinegar
1 teaspoon onion powder
1 teaspoon garlic powder
½ teaspoon sweet smoked paprika

The pickles, sauce, and relish market is huge, but you can make this excellent version at home by simply mixing together a handful of ingredients that you are likely to have already in your kitchen. It is guaranteed to take your homemade burgers to the next level.

1   Preheat the broiler to high.
2   Put the bacon on a baking sheet and place under the broiler for 5 minutes, or until crisp.
3   Mix together all the sauce ingredients.
4   Place the ground beef in a bowl and season with salt and pepper. Mix well with clean hands and form into 4 large burgers.
5   Heat the oil in a large frying pan and, when hot, add the burgers. Cook for 3 minutes on each side, then top each one with a slice of cheese, turn the heat down, and put a lid on the pan.
6   When the bacon is cooked, cut the burger buns in half and place under the broiler until lightly toasted.
7   Spread 2 spoonfuls of the sauce on the bottom half of the buns, then put the burgers on top followed by the bacon. Now add the tomato slices, pickle chips, and lettuce. Spread another 2 spoonfuls of the sauce on the remaining halves of the buns and place them on top.

Veal Scallopini with Mushroom Sauce

Serves 4

½ ounce dried porcini mushrooms

½ cup boiling water

½ cup all-purpose flour

4 veal cutlets (about 12 ounces in total)

2 tablespoons olive oil

2 tablespoons butter

2 large shallots, peeled and finely diced

2 garlic cloves, peeled and finely chopped

½ cup dry white wine

7 ounces cremini mushrooms, thickly sliced

¾ cup heavy cream

8 ounces Broccolini

½ cup cold water

1 tablespoon finely chopped flat-leaf parsley

Sea salt and freshly ground black pepper

Chef's tip

If you have leftover wine after making the sauce, pour it into ice cube trays and freeze for the next time you need a small quantity of alcohol to deglaze a pan or make a sauce.

I love cooking veal as an alternative to beef because it's very lean, extremely tender, and totally delicious. As the meat is so lean and the cutlets are so thin, be careful not to overcook them—a minute on each side is all it takes. The easy sauce that goes with them is great with cremini mushrooms, but you can swap them for baby bellas, wild mushrooms, or fresh porcini, if you can get hold of them.

1 Put the dried porcini into a small, heatproof bowl and pour the boiling water over them. Cover the bowl with plastic wrap and set aside.

2 Put the flour into a shallow dish. Season both sides of the veal with salt and pepper and coat each cutlet with flour.

3 Place a large nonstick frying pan over medium-high heat and add the oil. When hot, add the veal, then cook for 1 minute on each side. Transfer to a plate.

4 Put the pan back over medium heat, add the butter, and, when it has melted, add the shallots and cook for 2 minutes, until softened. Add the garlic and cook for an additional 1–2 minutes before pouring in the wine. Cook over high heat for 2 minutes, or until the liquid reduces by half.

5 Strain the mushroom liquid directly into the pan, then roughly chop the porcini mushrooms. Add them to the pan with the cremini mushrooms and cream. Season to taste and reduce to a sauce consistency, then return the veal to the pan.

6 Put the Broccolini into a pan with the cold water and a pinch of salt and pepper. Cook for 4–5 minutes, until the water has evaporated and the Broccolini is tender.

7 Spoon the veal and sauce onto plates and sprinkle with the parsley. Place the Broccolini alongside before serving.

Sticky Pork with Asian Greens

Serves 2

2 (10-ounce) thick pork chops
2 garlic cloves, peeled and crushed
2 tablespoons hoisin sauce
1 tablespoon Shaoxing rice wine
1 tablespoon brown sugar
1 tablespoon honey
1 teaspoon Chinese five-spice powder
1 tablespoon vegetable oil

For the greens

1 tablespoon vegetable oil
5 ounces snow peas and/or sugarsnap
   peas
5 ounces baby bok choy
2 tablespoons water
1 tablespoon soy sauce
Pinch of ground white pepper

If you have more time...

...leave the chops to marinate
in the sauce for longer, as the
ingredients will meld together
beautifully and really penetrate
the pork.

This sticky Asian marinade works brilliantly with pork chops, and all the ingredients for it are great to have in the pantry so you can easily whip up a satisfying midweek meal like this without much effort. Building a clever larder of sauces and spices is a great way to inject flavor into your meals without having to spend any extra time in the kitchen (see my advice for pantry basics on pages 6–7).

1 Preheat the oven to 400°F.
2 Using a sharp knife, trim the fat off each pork chop.
3 Combine the garlic, hoisin sauce, rice wine, sugar, honey, and five-spice powder in a shallow bowl. Add the pork chops and let them marinate for a few minutes.
4 Place a large, ovenproof frying pan over medium heat. When hot, add the oil. Scrape as much marinade as possible off the chops, then put them into the pan and cook for 1–2 minutes on each side. Add the remaining marinade to the pan and place in the oven for 6–8 minutes.
5 Heat a large dry wok until smoking hot. Add the oil and stir-fry the peas for 1 minute. Add the bok choy with the water, soy sauce, and a pinch of white pepper. Stir-fry for another 1–2 minutes.
6 Remove the pork from the oven and serve with the stir-fried greens.

Juniper Venison Steaks with Quick-Braised Red Cabbage

Serves 2

1 teaspoon juniper berries

2 (7-ounce) venison steaks

1 tablespoon mild olive oil

⅓ cup port

1 cup chicken stock

1 teaspoon thyme leaves

1 tablespoon red wine jelly

2 tablespoon butter

Sea salt and freshly ground black
   pepper

For the braised red cabbage

3 tablespoons butter

1 small onion, peeled and finely diced

2 garlic cloves, peeled and finely
   chopped

1 tablespoon brown sugar

1 tablespoon red wine vinegar

⅓ cup red wine

10 ounces red cabbage, shredded

½ cup chicken stock

½ teaspoon pumpkin pie spice

Chef's tip

Resting meat might seem like
a poor use of time when you're
rushing to get food on the table,
but it will make all the difference to
the end result—rested meat is
more tender and so much juicier.

Traditionally, braised red cabbage is something you cook for an hour or two to serve with your festive turkey, but red cabbage is for life, not just for holidays! This quick-braised version takes about 15 minutes and has all the flavor of the slow-cook recipes, but with a bit more bite, as the cabbage isn't cooked for so long. It is a cracking accompaniment to venison, sausages, and roast pork, as well as turkey.

1. Preheat the oven to 400°F.

2. First make the red cabbage. Place a saucepan over medium heat and add 1½ tablespoons of the butter. When it has melted, add the onion and cook for 2 minutes before adding the garlic and cooking for an additional minute. Add the sugar, vinegar, wine, cabbage, chicken stock, and pumpkin pie spice. Bring to a gentle simmer and cook for 10–12 minutes, until the cabbage is tender.

3. Meanwhile, using a mortar and pestle, crush the juniper. Sprinkle over both sides of the venison and season with salt and pepper.

4. Place an ovenproof nonstick frying pan over high heat. When hot, add the oil, then the venison steaks, and brown for 1–2 minutes on each side, depending on their thickness. Transfer the frying pan to the oven for about 6 minutes for medium-rare steaks. Place the steaks on a warm plate to rest.

5. Put the pan back over the heat, keeping a towel wrapped around the handle, as it will be very hot. Deglaze the pan with the port and allow it to reduce by half.

6. Add the chicken stock and thyme and let that reduce by half too. Strain the mixture through a sieve, then pour it back into the pan. When hot, add the red wine jelly, allow it to melt, then stir in the butter. Season to taste and remove from the heat.

7. Check the cabbage, season with salt and pepper to taste, then stir in the remaining 1½ tablespoons butter.

8. Carve the venison into thick slices and place it on plates with the red cabbage. Spoon the port sauce over the meat to serve.

Korean-Style Lamb with Sesame Cucumber

Serves 2

6 lamb rack cutlets, bone in
2 tablespoons soy sauce
2 tablespoons mirin
1 tablespoon sesame oil
2 tablespoons gochujang chile paste
2 garlic cloves, peeled and crushed
1-inch piece of fresh ginger, peeled and finely grated
Shichimi togarashi (seven-spice powder) or black sesame seeds, to serve

For the sesame cucumber
1 large cucumber
2 tablespoons tahini
1½ tablespoons rice vinegar
1 tablespoon sesame oil
1 teaspoon superfine sugar
1 tablespoon toasted sesame seeds

Gochujang sauce is a fermented chile paste from Korea, and is hot, sweet, and pungent. It is available from many supermarkets and can be stirred into dipping sauces, soups, stews, and fried rice (as on page 176) for a unique kick. It also makes a great marinade for meat and fish, but it's really punchy stuff, so use less if you don't like things too hot.

1   Preheat the broiler to high. Line a roasting pan with foil.

2   Place a nonstick frying pan over high heat, then place the cutlets, fat side down, for 2–3 minutes, until the skin is golden and crisp. Remove from the pan and leave to cool.

3   Put the soy sauce, mirin, sesame oil, gochujang paste, garlic, and ginger in a large bowl and mix together. Add the lamb and coat in the marinade. Place on the prepared pan, fat side down, and broil for 7–8 minutes, turning halfway through the cooking time.

4   Meanwhile, cut the cucumber in half lengthwise and use a teaspoon to scoop out all the seeds. Cut the cucumber into thick sticks about 2 inches long.

5   Combine the tahini, vinegar, sesame oil, and sugar in a large bowl. Add the cucumber, then stir in the toasted sesame seeds and mix well.

6   Place the cutlets on plates and run a blowtorch over them, if you have one, until lightly charred in places. Add the cucumbers and sprinkle with a little togarashi to serve.

Mexican Beef and Jalapeño Quesadillas

Serves 4

2 tablespoons olive oil, plus extra for brushing
1 onion, peeled and diced
2 garlic cloves, peeled and crushed
1 pound ground beef
2 teaspoons paprika
2 teaspoons ground cumin
1 (14-ounce) can of diced tomatoes
1 (14-ounce) can of kidney beans, drained and rinsed
4 (10-inch) flour tortillas
3 ounces grated mozzarella cheese
3 ounces grated Cheddar cheese
4 spring onions, trimmed and sliced
¼ cup pickled jalapeño
Sea salt and freshly ground black pepper
Sour cream, to serve

For the salsa

4 tomatoes, diced
1 red onion, peeled and finely diced
Large handful of cilantro, roughly chopped
Juice of 1 lime

My kids love these chile quesadillas—they're always gone minutes after they hit the table. But my lot, especially Jack, like things particularly hot and spicy, so go easy on the jalapeños if you're feeding a more sensitive crowd, or leave them out altogether. Making the salsa from scratch might seem like an added hassle, but it's definitely worth it.

1 Preheat the oven to 425°F. Line two large baking sheets with parchment paper.

2 Place a large nonstick frying pan over high heat. Add the oil and onion and cook for 2–3 minutes, until the onion has softened. Add the garlic and cook for 2 minutes, then crumble in the ground beef. Cook over high heat for 4–5 minutes, until the beef is lightly browned.

3 Stir in the spices and cook for 1–2 minutes. Add the canned tomatoes, cook for 2 minutes, then remove from the heat. Stir in the kidney beans and season to taste.

4 Lightly brush one side of a tortilla with extra oil and place on a prepared sheet, oiled side down. Sprinkle a little cheese over one half and spread a quarter of the beef mixture on top. Scatter some spring onions, jalapeños, and cheese on top before folding over the tortilla. Repeat for the remaining tortillas.

5 Press them down firmly and place on the two highest shelves of the oven for 10–15 minutes, until golden brown.

6 While the quesadillas are cooking, mix all the salsa ingredients in a bowl and season to taste.

7 Remove the quesadillas from the oven and cut into wedges before serving with a dollop of sour cream and some salsa on the side.

Ground Lamb Curry

Serves 4

2 tablespoons ghee or vegetable oil

2 onions, peeled and finely chopped

5 garlic cloves, peeled and crushed

2-inch piece of fresh ginger, peeled
   and finely grated

1 teaspoon ground turmeric

1 tablespoon garam masala

1 teaspoon Kashmiri chili powder

4 cardamom pods

2 tablespoons tomato purée

1 pound ground lamb

2 cups lamb stock

1 (14-ounce) can of diced tomatoes

1 pound potatoes, peeled and cut
   into ½-inch dice

1 tablespoon methi (fenugreek) leaves
   (optional)

1⅓ cups frozen peas

Small handful of fresh cilantro, roughly
   chopped

1 green chile, seeded if you
   want a milder hit, thinly sliced

Given the timeframe, a regular, slow-cooked lamb curry is out of the question, but this ground lamb version is much quicker and no less tasty. Serve it with the Aromatic Saffron Pilaf on page 204 if time isn't an issue, or buy some naan bread or chapattis to mop up the sauce. Dried methi, or fenugreek, leaves are available from some supermarkets and specialty Indian or Middle Eastern shops, but leave them out if you can't get hold of them.

1   Place a large nonstick sauté pan over high heat. When hot, add the ghee or oil and the onions and cook for 5 minutes, or until lightly golden brown.

2   Add the garlic and ginger and stir for 2 minutes.

3   Reduce the heat, then add the turmeric, garam masala, chili powder, and cardamom pods and stir until aromatic.

4   Add the tomato purée and stir for an additional minute.

5   Add the lamb and stir for 2–3 minutes, breaking up the meat as it cooks.

6   Add the stock and diced tomatoes and bring to a simmer.

7   Add the potatoes and methi (if using) and cook for 10–15 minutes over high heat, until the sauce has thickened and the potatoes are cooked.

8   Stir in the peas and cook for 1 minute to warm through, then garnish with the cilantro and chile before serving with warm chapattis or parathas.

Pork Larb with Sticky Coconut Rice

Serves 2

2 tablespoons jasmine rice

2 tablespoons vegetable oil

14 ounces ground pork

1 teaspoon superfine sugar

2 tablespoons fish sauce

1 tablespoon soy sauce

Juice of 1–2 limes

2 Thai red chiles, seeded if you want a milder hit, thinly sliced

4 shallots, peeled and thinly sliced

4 spring onions, trimmed and thinly sliced at an angle

Large handful of cilantro leaves

Large handful of mint leaves

Round lettuce or Little Gem leaves, to serve

Sea salt

For the sticky coconut rice

1 cup jasmine rice

1 (14-ounce) can of coconut milk

Pinch of salt

Chef's tip

Filling the lettuce cups with the hot larb too early will make the leaves soggy, so get people to fill their own at the table.

My recent travels have taken me to the fascinating country of Laos, where the bold, aromatic food is full of fresh herbs and chiles. Larb, which roughly translates as "meat salad," is almost the national dish, and is served with sticky rice cupped in lettuce leaves. The Laotians like their food extremely spicy, but you can reduce the number of chiles if you don't like it too hot.

1 Toast the 2 tablespoons rice for 5 minutes in a dry frying pan over medium heat, or until golden brown. Using a mortar and pestle, grind the rice to a coarse powder.

2 For the coconut rice, put the 1 cup jasmine rice into a saucepan with the coconut milk and a pinch of salt. Place over medium-high heat and bring to a simmer, then reduce the heat to low, cover with a lid, and cook for 10–12 minutes.

3 Meanwhile, place a dry wok over high heat. When it begins to smoke, add the oil, then stir-fry the pork for 2 minutes, or until it begins to brown slightly.

4 Add the sugar, fish sauce, soy sauce, and lime juice and stir-fry for 5 minutes.

5 Add half the ground rice, the chiles, shallots, spring onions, and herbs and stir-fry for another minute.

6 Put the larb (pork mixture) into warm bowls and sprinkle with the remaining ground rice before serving with the coconut rice and lettuce leaves.

Veal Saltimbocca with Marsala Sauce

Serves 2

4 veal cutlets (about 12 ounces
   in total)
3½ ounces Taleggio cheese
8 sage leaves
4 thin slices of speck
7 ounces green beans
¼ cup all-purpose flour
4 tablespoons butter
Olive oil, for frying
½ cup Marsala wine
¾ cup chicken stock
Sea salt and freshly ground black
   pepper

If you have more time...
...make the Decadent Mashed
Potatoes on page 207; they go
brilliantly with the crisp saltimbocca
and rich Marsala sauce.

This is the Union Street Café (USC) version of saltimbocca alla Romana, a classic Italian dish of veal and sage leaves covered in prosciutto. Veal is ultra-lean, so wrapping it in the ham protects the meat from drying out while it's cooking. At USC, they use lightly smoked speck to wrap the cutlets, and they slip in a piece of Taleggio cheese for extra deliciousness. The Marsala sauce brings the whole thing together with a rich sweetness, creating a stunning dish in very little time.

1 Place each cutlet between two pieces of plastic wrap and gently flatten it with a meat mallet or rolling pin.

2 Cut the Taleggio into 4 equal pieces and put one on each of the cutlets, followed by 2 sage leaves. Wrap the cutlets in the slices of speck and put them in the fridge for 5 minutes.

3 Meanwhile, bring a kettle of water to a boil and slice the green beans.

4 Remove the veal from the fridge and dust each one with a little flour.

5 Place two large frying pans over high heat and, when hot, add 1 tablespoon of the butter and a little olive oil to each pan. When the butter has melted and is bubbling, place two cutlets in each pan, cheese side down, and cook for 3 minutes, or until golden and crisp.

6 Pour the boiled water into a saucepan, bring back to a boil, then cook the green beans for 3–4 minutes, until just tender.

7 Turn the cutlets over and cook for about another 30 seconds. Transfer them to a platter and keep warm.

8 Deglaze the pans with half of the Marsala in each, then pour the wine from one pan into the other and allow it to reduce to a glaze. Add the chicken stock and reduce to a sauce consistency. Stir through the remaining 2 tablespoons of butter, then season with salt and pepper to taste.

9 Serve the cutlets on warm plates with a pile of green beans and drizzle with the Marsala sauce.

Mustard and Herb Meatballs with Balsamic Glaze and Parmesan Cheese

Serves 4

½ cup whole milk

2 rosemary sprigs, leaves finely chopped

5 thyme sprigs, leaves picked

4 slices fresh white bread, crusts removed and quartered

1 pound ground beef

1 egg

1 tablespoon Dijon mustard

Mild olive oil, for frying

½ cup aged balsamic vinegar

3½ ounces arugula

3 tablespoons extra virgin olive oil

Juice of ½ lemon

¾ ounce Parmesan cheese

Sea salt and freshly ground black pepper

If you have more time...

...make the Blood Orange, Radicchio, and Fennel Salad (see page 196) to go with these tasty meatballs.

There are three meatball recipes in this book (see also pages 30 and 175), and they are very different from each other, but what they have in common is that they are all very quick to make from scratch and absolutely delicious. It always pays to double the recipe so that you can put a second batch in the freezer for an instant meal in the future.

1 Pour the milk into a shallow bowl and stir in the rosemary and thyme. Add the quartered bread and allow to soak.

2 Meanwhile, put the beef, egg, and mustard into a large bowl and season with salt and pepper.

3 With clean hands, rub the soaked bread to a smooth paste between your fingers, then add it to the beef. Mix everything together until well combined. Dipping your hands in water from time to time, divide the mixture into 24 equal pieces and roll them into walnut-sized meatballs.

4 Place a large nonstick frying pan over medium-high heat and, when hot, add a little oil. Add the meatballs to the pan in batches and cook for 4–5 minutes, turning occasionally, until golden brown on all sides and cooked through.

5 Transfer the meatballs to a platter, then pour the oil from the pan and deglaze with the balsamic vinegar. Cook for 2–3 minutes, until slightly reduced.

6 Meanwhile, put the arugula into a bowl, add the extra virgin olive oil and lemon juice, and toss well.

7 Drizzle the balsamic glaze over the meatballs and grate the Parmesan over the top. Serve with the dressed arugula and a crisp ciabatta loaf straight from the oven.

Rib Eye Steaks with Peppercorn Sauce

Serves 2

2 tablespoons olive oil

2 (8-ounce) rib eye steaks

4 thyme sprigs

2 tablespoons butter

1 shallot, peeled and finely diced

2 tablespoons green peppercorns

1 large garlic clove, peeled and finely chopped

¼ cup cognac

1 teaspoon Dijon mustard

¾ cup beef stock

2 dashes of Worcestershire sauce

⅔ cup heavy cream

Sea salt and freshly ground black pepper

Chef's tip

Always dry meat and fish thoroughly with paper towels before frying, as any moisture will slow down caramelization, and you risk overcooking the steak, chop, or fillet while trying to get a nice color.

If you have more time...

...serve with the Mustard Mash on page 207 or the Green Beans with Tarragon and Pine Nuts on page 200.

Many people order steaks when they go out to a restaurant, but they never cook them at home, which is just daft, if you ask me. Cooking a steak is incredibly easy—no prep, a few minutes basting with butter in a hot pan, and a few minutes to rest afterward, job done. And the sauce takes only a few minutes more to rustle up. The main thing is to buy a decent steak, as no amount of basting or smothering with sauce can make a rubbish steak taste anything but rubbish.

1 Place a large nonstick frying pan over high heat. Rub the olive oil over the steaks and season liberally with salt and pepper. When the pan is smoking hot, add the steaks and cook for 2–3 minutes on each side if you like your steaks medium-rare (or longer for desired doneness).

2 Remove the pan from the heat, then add the thyme and butter, and baste, baste, baste the steaks for at least a minute. Turn them over and baste again. Transfer the steaks and thyme to a warm plate and leave to rest.

3 Return the pan to medium heat, add the shallot, and cook for 2–3 minutes, until softened. Add the green peppercorns and garlic and cook for 1–2 minutes.

4 Pour in the cognac and flambé carefully. Add the mustard, beef stock, and Worcestershire sauce, stir well, and increase the heat to high. Let the stock reduce by half before adding the cream. Allow it to cook for another few minutes, until the cream has thickened.

5 Put the rested steaks on serving plates, making sure to pour any resting juices into the sauce. Stir the sauce well and season to taste before pouring it over the steaks and serving with green vegetables.

Roast Pork Chops with Crushed New Potatoes and Lettuce and Apple Salad

Serves 2

1 tablespoon vegetable oil
2 (10-ounce) thick pork chops
2 tablespoons butter
1 garlic clove, peeled and crushed with
    the blade of a chef's knife
2 thyme sprigs
Sea salt and freshly ground black
    pepper

For the crushed potatoes
10 ounces new potatoes
2 ounces smoked bacon lardons or
    pancetta
2 spring onions, trimmed and thinly
    sliced

For the dressing
¼ cup olive oil
2 tablespoons white wine vinegar
½ teaspoon grainy mustard
Pinch of salt

For the salad
2 Little Gem lettuces, leaves separated
½ Honey Crisp or other sweet apple,
    peeled and shaved with a vegetable
    peeler
1 tablespoon finely chopped chives

Time-saving tip
Make double or triple the recipe for
this simple salad dressing
and keep it in a jar or bottle to save
time when you next need
to dress a salad.

Make sure you buy thick-cut chops for this recipe and take them out of the fridge at least five minutes before cooking, ideally longer, as bringing them nearer to room temperature will prevent the meat from drying out, which can be a real danger with pork. Dressing the potatoes while they are still warm means that they really absorb the flavors of the bacon, onions, and vinaigrette, and will consequently taste much better.

1   Preheat the oven to 400°F.
2   Bring a kettle of water to a boil, then pour it into a saucepan. Season with salt and bring back to a boil over medium-high heat. Add the potatoes and cook for 15 minutes, until tender.
3   Place a large ovenproof frying pan over high heat. Drizzle the vegetable oil over the pork chops and season with salt and pepper. When the pan is hot, add the chops and cook for 1–2 minutes on each side. Add the butter and, when foaming, baste the meat with it. Add the garlic and thyme, then transfer the pan to the oven for 6–8 minutes. When the chops are cooked through, transfer to a warm plate and allow to rest.
4   Meanwhile, place a frying pan over medium-high heat and add the bacon lardons. Cook for 5–8 minutes, until crisp and golden. Drain on paper towels.
5   Combine the dressing ingredients in a bowl and whisk together.
6   When the potatoes are cooked, drain in a colander, then transfer to a bowl and crush lightly with a fork. Stir in the spring onions and crispy bacon. Drizzle over two-thirds of the dressing, then stir well and season with salt and pepper.
7   Combine the salad ingredients in a bowl, add the remaining dressing, and toss well.
8   Drizzle the pork chops with some of the pan juices and serve with a generous spoonful of the crushed potatoes and the salad on the side.

Lamb Sirloin Roast with Creamed Cannellini Beans

Serves 2

2 (8-ounce) lamb sirloin roasts

2 tablespoons olive oil

2 tablespoons butter

¾ cup lamb stock

6 ounces Broccolini or green beans, trimmed

2 anchovies in olive oil, finely chopped

½ cup water

Sea salt and freshly ground black pepper

For the creamed cannellini beans

1 tablespoon olive oil

1 shallot, peeled and finely diced

2 garlic cloves, peeled and finely chopped

2 rosemary sprigs, leaves finely chopped

2 (14-ounce) cans of cannellini beans, drained and rinsed

½ cup heavy cream

This is one of those meals that punches above its weight—the deliciousness of the finished dish far outweighs the amount of effort put into creating it. The creamy, rosemary-flavored beans are an excellent accompaniment to the lamb and Broccolini, but you could also serve them with a juicy steak or some crisp chicken thighs, or simply on toast like posh baked beans.

1   Preheat the oven to 400°F.

2   Score the fat on the lamb with a sharp knife and season with salt and pepper. Place an ovenproof nonstick frying pan over high heat. When hot, add 1 tablespoon of the oil, then place the lamb in the pan and cook for 3–4 minutes on each side. Transfer the pan to the oven for 8–10 minutes.

3   Meanwhile, make the creamed cannellini. Heat the olive oil in a saucepan over medium heat. Add the shallot and cook for 2–3 minutes, until softened. Add the garlic and rosemary and cook for another 2 minutes. Stir in the cannellini beans and cream, then cook over medium heat for 5 minutes. Season to taste.

4   Remove the lamb from the oven. Add the butter and baste the lamb for 2 minutes. Transfer the lamb to a warm plate to rest.

5   Place the pan over high heat and add the stock. Allow to boil and reduce for 5 minutes, until the sauce thickens a little.

6   Put the Broccolini into another frying pan with the remaining 1 tablespoon of olive oil, the anchovies, and water. Bring to a boil and cook for about 5 minutes. Season to taste.

7   Divide the cannellini beans and Broccolini between two plates, then carve the lamb into thick slices and lay them on top. Pour the sauce over the meat before serving.

Meat-Free Mains

Lentil Burgers

Serves 4

4 tablespoons olive oil

1 onion, peeled and finely chopped

2 garlic cloves, peeled and finely chopped

2 jalapeño chiles, seeded for a milder hit, finely chopped

1 red pepper, seeded and diced

1 teaspoon ground cumin

1 teaspoon sweet smoked paprika

1 (14-ounce) can of chickpeas, drained and rinsed

1¼ cups cooked green lentils

½ cup fresh breadcrumbs

1 egg, lightly beaten

¼ cup all-purpose flour, for dusting

4 slices of Cheddar cheese

Sea salt and freshly ground black pepper

To serve

½ cup mayonnaise

2 teaspoons chipotle chiles in adobo

1 tablespoon yellow mustard

4 whole wheat burger buns, split open

Little Gem lettuce leaves

2 large pickles, thinly sliced lengthwise

1 ripe avocado, peeled, pitted, and thinly sliced

Chef's tip

To seed a bell pepper, chop the stalk off, then stand it on the cut end and slice from top to bottom, avoiding the seeds.

In my restaurant kitchens, we have spent a lot of time trying to develop the ultimate vegan burger, and I think this is a pretty damn good one. The combination of lentils and blitzed chickpeas gives it an authentic texture, and the spiced peppers and onions give it proper depth of flavor. Leave out the cheese, sauce, and egg if you're vegan.

1 Preheat the oven to 400°F.

2 Place a nonstick frying pan over high heat and add 2 tablespoons of the olive oil. When hot, add the onion and cook for 2–3 minutes, until softened. Add the garlic, chiles, and red pepper and cook for an additional 2–3 minutes. Stir in the cumin, paprika, and a big pinch of salt, then remove from the heat.

3 Put the chickpeas into a food processor and tip in the onion mixture. Pulse just until the mixture combines— you want to retain some texture. Transfer this mixture to a large bowl.

4 Add the lentils, breadcrumbs, and beaten egg to the bowl, season with salt and pepper, and mix well with clean hands. Divide the mixture into 4 equal-sized burgers. Dust both sides with the flour, brushing off any excess.

5 Place a large nonstick frying pan over high heat and add the remaining 2 tablespoons of olive oil. When hot, add the burgers and cook for 2 minutes on each side. Transfer them to a baking sheet and top each one with a slice of cheese. Place in the oven for 5 minutes. When cooked, remove from the oven and switch the broiler on.

6 Meanwhile, mix together the mayonnaise, chipotle chiles in adobo, and mustard.

7 Place the hamburger buns, cut side up, under the broiler for 1–2 minutes, until lightly toasted. Spread both halves with some of the mayonnaise mixture, then place the lettuce leaves on each bottom half, followed by a burger. Top with the pickles, avocado, and bun lids, and serve straight away.

Quick Butternut Squash and Chickpea Curry

Serves 4

3 tablespoons vegetable oil

1 tablespoon black mustard seeds

1 tablespoon cumin seeds

Small handful of curry leaves

1 large onion, peeled and finely
   chopped

1 pound peeled butternut squash

4 garlic cloves, peeled and crushed

1-inch piece of fresh ginger, peeled
   and finely grated

1 heaping teaspoon ground turmeric

1 heaping teaspoon paprika

2 heaping teaspoons ground coriander

2½ cups vegetable stock

1 (14-ounce) can of coconut cream

2 (14-ounce) cans of chickpeas,
   drained and rinsed

3 large handfuls of baby spinach

Sea salt and freshly ground black
   pepper

If you have more time...
...make a double batch of the
curry, as it will taste even better
the next day.

This straightforward, warming curry packs a hearty punch for vegans, vegetarians, and people trying to eat less meat. It is wonderful when you first cook it, but even better a couple of days later, as time allows the spices to blend together and become more mellow and rounded.

1   Place a large nonstick saucepan over high heat and add the oil. When hot, add the mustard seeds, cumin seeds, and curry leaves, then stir and cook for 30 seconds.

2   Add the onion and cook for 4–5 minutes, until softened and beginning to brown.

3   Meanwhile, cut the butternut squash into ½-inch cubes.

4   Add the garlic and ginger to the pan and cook for 1–2 minutes.

5   Reduce the heat a little, then stir in the dried spices and cook for 1 minute. Pour in the stock and bring to a boil.

6   Add the squash and coconut cream, stir well, then bring back to a boil and cook for 10–12 minutes, until the squash is tender and the sauce has thickened.

7   Stir in the chickpeas, season well with salt and pepper, then stir in the spinach. Serve the curry in warm bowls with plain rice, Aromatic Saffron Pilaf (page 204), or some naan bread.

Truffle Mushrooms with Cheesy Polenta

Serves 4

1½ pounds mixed mushrooms, such as cremini, portobello, or oyster
3 tablespoons olive oil
4 garlic cloves, peeled and finely chopped
1¾ ounces porcini and truffle paste (See Chef's tip, below)
1 cup heavy cream
1 tablespoon finely chopped tarragon
1 tablespoon thyme leaves
Truffle oil, to serve

For the cheesy polenta

1½ quarts vegetable stock
2 rosemary sprigs, leaves finely chopped
7 ounces instant/quick-cook polenta
1¾ ounces Parmesan cheese, finely grated, plus extra to serve
3½ ounces Taleggio cheese, cut into cubes
3 tablespoons butter
Sea salt and freshly ground black pepper

Chef's tip

Porcini and truffle paste can be found in Italian delis and online specialty shops.

Chefs often look to mushrooms when they are trying to re-create the depth of flavor that meat brings to cooking. They are full of umami and earthy notes that other vegetables simply don't have. Here the flavor of the mushrooms is intensified by stirring through some porcini and truffle paste during the cooking and drizzling truffle oil over the top to finish.

1   Pour the stock for the polenta into a large saucepan and place over medium heat.
2   Meanwhile, cut the various mushrooms into equal 1-inch pieces.
3   Place a large nonstick frying pan over high heat and add half the oil. When hot, add half the mushrooms and cook for 2–3 minutes, until golden brown. Drain on paper towels, then heat the remaining oil and cook the rest of the mushrooms. Set aside on paper towels.
4   Add the garlic to the pan and cook for 1 minute before adding the porcini paste, cream, and herbs. Cook for 3–4 minutes over medium heat, until the sauce becomes very thick.
5   Meanwhile, add the rosemary to the hot stock, increase the heat, and pour in the polenta. Cook for 3–5 minutes, until tender. Stir in the Parmesan and Taleggio and season to taste. Finally, stir in the butter until it has melted. Keep warm.
6   Add the mushrooms to the cream sauce and bring back to a simmer. Season to taste.
7   Serve the polenta in bowls with the mushroom sauce spooned over the top. Add a drizzle of truffle oil, a twist of black pepper, and a sprinkling of Parmesan before serving.

Sichuan Sesame Noodles

Serves 4

1 onion, peeled and thinly sliced

7 ounces cremini mushrooms, halved

7 ounces oyster mushrooms, torn into equal pieces

7 ounces snowpeas, sliced in half at an angle

7 ounces bok choy, cut into 3-inch lengths

4 spring onions, trimmed and thinly sliced at an angle

1 tablespoon vegetable oil

2 tablespoons sesame oil

1 teaspoon Sichuan peppercorns, crushed

1½ pounds fresh udon noodles, cooked

For the sesame and peanut sauce

3 tablespoons tahini

2 tablespoons crunchy peanut butter

¼ cup soy sauce

4 garlic cloves, peeled and grated

2-inch piece of fresh ginger, peeled and grated

2 tablespoons rice vinegar

½ cup coconut milk

½ cup water

To serve

½ cucumber, halved lengthwise and thinly sliced

¼ cup toasted sesame seeds

Chili oil

Sichuan pepper is a citrusy, vibrant variety of pepper from China that has a lip-tingling, mouth-numbing effect when you eat it. It elevates this simple bowl of noodles to something that packs a little more punch than your average midweek stir-fry. Udon are thick Japanese noodles that you can buy ready-cooked, but you can use whatever noodles you have in the pantry.

1　Make the sesame and peanut sauce by combining all the ingredients for it in a bowl.

2　Prepare all the vegetables as specified for the stir-fry, and also the cucumber that will be needed to serve.

3　Place a large nonstick wok over high heat until it begins to smoke. Add the vegetable and sesame oils, then add the onion and peppercorns and stir-fry for 1–2 minutes. Add the mushrooms and snow peas and stir-fry for another 2 minutes.

4　Add the noodles and the sesame and peanut sauce and stir-fry for 2–3 minutes. Add the bok choy and cook for another 1–2 minutes, until the noodles are piping hot and the sauce has reduced. Remove from the heat and stir in the spring onions.

5　Pile the stir-fry into bowls and top each with a spoonful of sesame seeds, a drizzle of chili oil, and a small handful of sliced cucumber.

Barbecued Mushrooms with Fennel Slaw and Onion Rings

Serves 2

½ cup barbecue sauce
2 teaspoons chipotle paste
4 portobello mushrooms, stalks
  removed
Vegetable oil, for frying

For the fennel slaw

3 ounces fennel, thinly sliced
3 ounces red cabbage, finely shredded
3 ounces carrot, grated
3 tablespoons mayonnaise
1 tablespoon white wine vinegar
Sea salt and freshly ground black
  pepper

For the onion rings

1¼ cups self-rising flour
1 teaspoon dried thyme
1 teaspoon garlic granules
1 cup cold sparkling water
1 small onion, peeled and thickly sliced
  into rings

If you have more time...

...cook the mushrooms on a hot barbecue with some corn on the cob to complete the feast. You can't beat the flavor that real charcoal adds.

What many vegetarians and vegans miss is the smoke and char of a barbecue, but there are some great veg that barbecue brilliantly, such as corn on the cob, asparagus, cauliflower steaks, peppers, and mushrooms. The large portobello mushrooms used here are glazed with barbecue sauce and smoky chipotle paste, then charred on a smoking hot grill pan to bring out those barbecue flavors. Serve with the onion rings and fennel slaw for the full effect. To make this recipe vegan, use vegan mayonnaise in the slaw.

1 Preheat the oven to 400°F. Place a grill pan over high heat.

2 Mix the barbecue sauce and chipotle paste together in a bowl. Using a pastry brush, coat both sides of the mushrooms with the sauce mixture. Put the mushrooms on the griddle for 2–3 minutes on each side, until they have charred lines.

3 Meanwhile, put all the vegetables for the slaw into a large bowl with the mayonnaise and vinegar. Season with salt and pepper, stir well, and set aside.

4 Transfer the mushrooms to a roasting pan along with any barbecue sauce remaining in the bowl. Place in the oven for 10–12 minutes.

5 Half-fill a small pan with vegetable oil and place over high heat.

6 Meanwhile, put the flour, thyme, and garlic into a bowl and season with salt and pepper. Whisk in the sparkling water to make a batter, then add the onion rings and stir carefully to coat.

7 Once the oil has reached 350–375°F, or a drop of batter sizzles instantly, carefully add four or five onion rings at a time and cook for 2–3 minutes, until golden brown on both sides. Drain on paper towels and cook the remaining rings in the same way.

8 Divide the mushrooms, slaw, and onion rings between serving plates. Sprinkle the rings with a little extra salt before serving.

Roasted Cauliflower with Israeli Couscous, Harissa Oil, and Lime Crème Fraîche

Serves 4

2 tablespoons olive oil
1 teaspoon ground turmeric
1 cauliflower, divided into large florets
1 cup Israeli or pearl couscous
Large handful of mint leaves, roughly
   chopped
Sea salt and freshly ground black
   pepper

For the harissa oil
2 tablespoons rose harissa
¼ cup olive oil

For the lime crème fraîche
⅔ cup crème fraîche
Zest and juice of 1 lime

To serve
Small handful of cilantro leaves
Large handful of crispy fried onions

Roasted cauliflower is nothing like the watery, slightly bitter-tasting boiled variety. It has a complex caramelized flavor that transforms it from a boring side veg into a stunning main course in its own right. Finish it with pungent harissa oil, lime crème fraîche, and a handful of those incredibly moreish crispy fried onions that you can buy in supermarkets.

1   Preheat the oven to 450°F.
2   Put the olive oil and turmeric into a large bowl, season with salt and pepper, and stir well to combine. Add the cauliflower and, using clean hands, toss until lightly coated in the yellow oil.
3   Tip the florets into a roasting pan and place on the top shelf of the oven for 10 minutes.
4   Meanwhile, cook the couscous according to the package instructions. When ready, stir in the chopped mint and season with salt and pepper. Cover with a lid and set aside until needed.
5   Combine the harissa and olive oil in a bowl and mix well. Set aside until needed.
6   Remove the pan from the oven and turn the cauliflower florets over. Return to the oven for an additional 5 minutes, or until cooked through and beginning to char.
7   Combine the crème fraîche, lime zest, and lime juice in a bowl, then taste, adding more lime juice if necessary.
8   When the cauliflower is ready, divide the florets among four plates and add a spoonful of the minted couscous and lime crème fraîche to each one. Spoon the harissa oil over the cauliflower and sprinkle with the cilantro leaves and crispy fried onions before serving.

Beet, Thyme, and Goat Cheese Tart with Pear and Arugula Salad

Serves 4

1 (17.3-ounce) package of frozen puff pastry, defrosted
1 cup cream cheese
½ cup sweet onion jam or chutney
14 ounces cooked beets
2 teaspoons thyme leaves
1 teaspoon nigella seeds
4 ounces soft goat cheese
1 tablespoon runny honey
1 egg, lightly beaten
Sea salt and freshly ground black pepper

For the pear and arugula salad
½ cup shelled walnuts
4 ounces arugula leaves
1 small ripe pear, cored and sliced
3 tablespoons extra virgin olive oil
1½ tablespoons white balsamic vinegar

Ready-made pastry is a brilliant thing to have in the fridge or freezer for quick tarts like this one. Yes, it's possible to make your own puff pastry, but it will take you two hours or so, and store-bought, all-butter puff is pretty good these days. Once you have tried this beet and goat cheese version, follow the same general method but with different toppings, such as marinated tomatoes, sautéed mushrooms, or caramelized onions.

1 Preheat the oven to 425°F. Line two baking sheets with parchment paper.

2 Place the walnuts on a separate small baking sheet and toast in the oven for 5 minutes. Set aside until needed.

3 Using a sharp knife and an 8- to 9-inch round plate or bowl, cut a circle out of each pastry sheet. Place the circles on the prepared sheets and prick the middle of each several times with a fork.

4 Mix the cream cheese and onion chutney together, then spread half the mixture over each circle, leaving a 1-inch border.

5 Using a mandoline, cut the beet into thin slices. Arrange them over the chutney in slightly overlapping circles.

6 Sprinkle with the thyme leaves, nigella seeds, and chunks of goat cheese, drizzle with the honey, and season with salt and pepper. Brush the edges of the pastry with the beaten egg, then place in the oven on the two highest shelves for 15–20 minutes, until golden and crisp.

7 Meanwhile, put the arugula and pear into a large bowl and season with salt and pepper. Whisk together the oil and vinegar, then pour over the salad and mix well. Roughly chop the walnuts and scatter them over the salad.

8 Remove the tarts from the oven and cut into wedges. Serve with the arugula salad on the side.

Vegetable Stir-Fry

Serves 2

1 carrot, halved lengthwise and sliced
   at an angle
5 ounces baby corn, cut in half at an
   angle
1 yellow squash, halved lengthwise
   and sliced at an angle
2 garlic cloves, peeled and finely
   chopped
1-inch piece of fresh ginger, peeled
   and grated
5 ounces bok choy, sliced
5 ounces asparagus, trimmed and cut
   into 1-inch pieces at an angle
7 ounces oyster mushrooms
2 spring onions, trimmed and thinly
   sliced at an angle
1 tablespoon vegetable oil
1 tablespoon sesame oil
2 tablespoons soy sauce
2 tablespoons oyster sauce
1 tablespoon honey
1 teaspoon cornstarch
Cooked rice, to serve

Time-saving tip
Rather than snapping off the woody
parts of the asparagus one by one,
use a chef's knife to cut them off in
one fell swoop while they are still
bunched in the elastic band.

**Making a stir-fry is a quick, hot business, and this
veg-only version should take around five minutes from
start to finish. Any longer than this and the veg will be
overcooked and unappetizing, so get all the prep done
before you start and you will be ready to add each of
the vegetables as and when you need to. Speed is
definitely of the essence, so measure out the oils and
sauces in advance too.**

1 Prepare all the vegetables before you start cooking.
   Place a wok over high heat until smoking hot. Add the
   oils, then stir-fry the carrot and corn for 1–2 minutes.
2 Add the squash, garlic, and ginger and stir-fry for
   2 minutes before adding the bok choy, asparagus, and
   oyster mushrooms. Pour in the soy sauce, oyster
   sauce, and honey and stir-fry for another 1–2 minutes.
3 Mix the cornstarch with 3 tablespoons water, add to the
   wok, and stir well. Add the spring onions and serve
   immediately with rice.

Corn and Zucchini Fritters with Tomato, Avocado, and Arugula Salad

Serves 4

2 ears corn on the cob

2 tablespoons olive oil, plus extra for pan-frying

4 spring onions, trimmed and thinly sliced

1 green chile, seeded if you want a milder hit, finely chopped

2 eggs, separated

½ cup whole milk

7 ounces zucchini, grated

½ cup self-rising flour

Small handful of fresh basil, chopped

3 ounces Cheddar cheese, grated

3 ounces mozzarella cheese, grated

2 ounces feta cheese, crumbled

Zest of 1 lemon

Sea salt and freshly ground black pepper

For the salad

7 ounces cherry tomatoes, halved

3½ ounces arugula leaves

1 ripe avocado, peeled, pitted, and sliced

1 tablespoon white balsamic vinegar

2 tablespoons extra virgin olive oil

Relaxed, tasty foods, like these corn and zucchini fritters, are ideal for a brunch or weekend lunch. Stripping the corn from the cobs might seem like a hassle, but raw corn will color and char far more than the wet-from-the-can variety. If you're really pressed for time, of course you can used canned corn, but make sure you drain and dry it thoroughly so it doesn't add any water to the batter.

1 Preheat the oven to 250°F.

2 Remove the corn kernels from the cobs by standing each cob upright and running a sharp knife down the sides.

3 Place a large nonstick frying pan over high heat. When hot, add the oil and corn and cook for 2–3 minutes, until the corn begins to char lightly. Add the spring onions and chile and cook for an additional 2 minutes. Remove from the heat and leave to cool slightly.

4 Put the egg yolks and milk into a bowl. Put the egg whites into a separate bowl and whisk until firm peaks form.

5 Squeeze any excess liquid from the zucchini and add it to the egg yolks along with the cooked corn mixture. Add the flour, basil, cheeses, and lemon zest. Season with salt and pepper, stir well, then gently fold in the egg whites.

6 Place two large nonstick frying pans over medium-high heat and pour a thin layer of olive oil into each one. When hot, place two large, separate spoonfuls of the corn mixture in each pan. Cook for 2 minutes on each side, or until golden and crisp. When ready, carefully transfer the fritters to a baking sheet and place in the oven to keep warm. Cook the remaining mixture in the same way.

7 Put all the salad ingredients into a bowl and mix well. Serve the hot corn fritters with a little salad on the side.

Spicy Smoked Tofu Lettuce Cups

Serves 2

2 tablespoons vegetable oil
1 tablespoon sesame oil
1 onion, peeled and diced
4 garlic cloves, peeled and crushed
9 ounces baby corn, thickly sliced
9 ounces portobello mushrooms, diced
2 tablespoons Shaoxing rice wine
14 ounces smoked tofu, crumbled
3 ounces water chestnuts, roughly
  chopped
3 tablespoons soy sauce
2 tablespoons sriracha sauce
1 tablespoon rice vinegar
2 large handfuls of bean sprouts
Large handful of cilantro leaves,
  roughly chopped

To serve

2 iceberg or round lettuce leaves,
  or 4 Little Gem leaves
1 red chile, seeded if you want
  a milder hit, thinly sliced
Handful of crispy fried onions

Chef's tip

Don't put the tofu mixture into
the lettuce cups too soon or the
leaves will become too soggy
to lift to your mouth.

Crumbled smoked tofu is a brilliant starting point for many vegan dishes—it has a great texture for scrambles, stir-fries, and salads, and the smoky flavor adds a depth that can sometimes be lacking in vegan food. Add some aromatics, some Asian veg, and this great combination of Chinese flavors, and you have a winning meat-free main course in under 30 minutes.

1   Place a large nonstick wok over high heat. When smoking hot, add the oils, then the onion, and stir-fry for 1–2 minutes. Add the garlic and baby corn and stir-fry for 1–2 minutes. Add the mushrooms and rice wine and stir-fry for another 2 minutes.

2   Sprinkle the tofu into the pan and stir in the water chestnuts. Add the soy sauce, sriracha, and rice vinegar and stir-fry for 1–2 minutes before adding the bean sprouts. Stir-fry for an additional minute, remove from the heat, then stir in the cilantro.

3   Serve the tofu mixture in bowls with the lettuce leaves on the side. Sprinkle with the red chile and crispy onions before serving.

Tofu and Vegetable Laksa

Serves 4

2–3 tablespoons Thai red curry paste

1 tablespoon sriracha sauce

2 tablespoons soy sauce

2½ cups vegetable stock

1 (14-ounce) can of coconut milk

1 cup coconut cream

2 teaspoons lemongrass paste

2 tablespoons fish sauce (omit for vegetarians)

7–10 ounces medium egg noodles

3½ ounces cremini mushrooms, halved

7 ounces baby zucchini, thickly sliced at an angle

7 ounces fried tofu puffs, cut in half

7 ounces snow peas

1 (8-ounce) can of bamboo shoots, drained

Juice of 1 lime

2 large handfuls of bean sprouts

To serve

Sliced red chile, seeded for a milder hit

Fresh cilantro

Unlike regular tofu, which is dense and quite difficult to infuse with flavor, the fried tofu puffs used here are like absorbent pillows that take in all the lovely spiciness of the broth. You can buy tofu puffs from Asian supermarkets and specialty websites, but if you can't get hold of any, shallow-fry some cubes of smoked tofu until crispy, then add them to the saucepan at the very end.

1 Make the broth by putting the red curry paste, sriracha, soy sauce, vegetable stock, coconut milk, coconut cream, lemongrass paste, and fish sauce (if using) into a saucepan and placing it over medium heat.

2 Bring a kettle of water to a boil, then pour it into a second saucepan and return to a boil. Add the noodles and cook according to the package instructions until tender. Drain well and divide them among four serving bowls.

3 Once the broth is simmering, add the mushrooms and zucchini to it and cook for 2 minutes. Add the tofu puffs, snow peas, and bamboo shoots and cook for another 2 minutes.

4 Taste the broth and add some lime juice to taste.

5 Ladle the broth and vegetables into the bowls containing the noodles. Add a small handful of bean sprouts to each bowl and serve garnished with the red chile and cilantro.

Pea, Basil, and Goat Cheese Omelet with Shaved Asparagus and Arugula Salad

Serves 4

7 ounces frozen peas

1½ tablespoons butter

Small handful of basil leaves, roughly chopped

8 large eggs, beaten

5-ounce goat cheese log, thickly sliced

¾ ounce Parmesan cheese, grated

Sea salt and freshly ground black pepper

For the salad

8 ounces asparagus, trimmed

Large handful of arugula leaves

Juice of ½ lemon

3 tablespoons olive oil

A basic omelet has to be the ultimate single-ingredient fast food because it can be on the plate within a couple of minutes of cracking the first egg. This pea, basil, and goat cheese version shouldn't take that much longer, but it is worth exercising a little patience when it goes under the broiler—a bit of color on the goat cheese will make the whole thing really sing.

1   Preheat the broiler to high.

2   Put the peas into a colander and hold them under running tepid water for about a minute. This will defrost them without cooking them.

3   Place a large ovenproof frying pan over medium-high heat and add the butter. When hot, add the peas, shake the pan, and cook for 1–2 minutes.

4   Add the basil and stir well before pouring in the beaten eggs, then cook for 2–3 minutes, until the omelet is beginning to set on the bottom.

5   Meanwhile, prepare the salad. Using a mandoline or vegetable peeler, slice the asparagus lengthwise into very fine shavings and place them in a bowl with the arugula. Whisk the lemon juice, olive oil, and a pinch of salt in a small bowl, then pour this dressing over the salad and toss well.

6   Dot the goat cheese slices over the omelet, sprinkle with the Parmesan, and season with salt and pepper. Place the frying pan under the broiler for 1–2 minutes, until the eggs are set on top and the goat cheese has begun to brown.

7   Transfer the omelet to a board or plate, slice into wedges, and serve with the asparagus and arugula salad.

Pasta, Rice, and Grains

Cacio e Pepe with Parmesan Crisps

Serves 2

2 ounces Parmesan cheese, finely
grated

7 ounces bucatini

1½ teaspoons black peppercorns

7 tablespoons butter

¾ ounce pecorino cheese, finely
grated

Sea salt

In several Italian dialects *cacio e pepe* **translates as "cheese and pepper," and that's essentially all that goes into this sauce. The magic ingredient that binds them together is the pasta cooking water. It is full of starch, which emulsifies with the butter and helps the sauce cling to the pasta. The Parmesan crisps are optional, but such an easy and impressive way to finish the dish.**

1 Preheat the oven to 400°F. Line a baking sheet with parchment paper.

2 To make the crisps, take half the Parmesan and place it in four equal piles on the prepared sheet. Place on a high shelf in the oven for 10–12 minutes, until the Parmesan has turned golden brown. Set aside.

3 Bring a kettle of water to a boil. Half-fill a saucepan with it, season with salt, and return to a boil. (It's important to add just enough water to cover the pasta so that the water will become as starchy as possible.) Add the pasta, stir well, and cook for 10 minutes, or until al dente.

4 Meanwhile, toast the peppercorns in a dry frying pan until aromatic. Using a mortar and pestle, grind them coarsely.

5 Place a large sauté pan over medium heat and melt the butter in it. Add the ground pepper and let the butter foam, then add a ladleful of the pasta water and bring to a boil. Swirl the pan or whisk the contents to emulsify the sauce.

6 Remove the pasta from the water with tongs and add it to the sauté pan with a second ladleful of the water and the remaining Parmesan. Stir well to coat, and add more pasta water if needed.

7 Add the pecorino and salt, tossing the pan to combine.

8 Serve in bowls with the Parmesan crisps crumbled over the top.

Tomato, Mascarpone, and Pancetta Rigatoni

Serves 4

3 tablespoons olive oil

8 ounces diced pancetta or smoked bacon

1 large onion, peeled and finely diced

3 garlic cloves, peeled and finely chopped

1 teaspoon Italian seasoning

3 ounces oil-packed sun-dried tomatoes, roughly chopped

1 (14-ounce) can of diced tomatoes

¾ cup chicken stock

7 ounces mascarpone cheese

14 ounces rigatoni

¾ ounce Parmesan cheese, finely grated, plus extra to serve

Small handful of basil leaves, roughly chopped

Sea salt and freshly ground black pepper

Chef's tip

Go to a good Italian deli and stock up on pancetta or bacon lardons to cut and store in the fridge (for up to a month), or freeze it in portions to use later. It's so handy for rustling up carbonara or other pasta sauces like this one at the last minute.

Here we have a tasty midweek supper that uses lots of pantry and fridge ingredients that have a relatively long shelf life—canned tomatoes, pancetta, mascarpone—making it a top standby recipe to feed your hungry family. If you leave out the pancetta and switch the chicken stock for vegetable bouillon or water, this becomes a really tasty, meat-free pasta sauce or base for pizza or vegetarian lasagna.

1   Place a large sauté pan over medium-high heat and add the oil. When hot, add the pancetta and cook for 3–4 minutes, until crisp and golden. Remove a big spoonful from the pan and drain on paper towels, then set aside to use as garnish.

2   Add the onion to the pan and cook until softened, then add the garlic and cook for 2 minutes.

3   Stir in the Italian seasoning, both lots of tomatoes, the chicken stock, and mascarpone. Bring to a gentle simmer and cook for 10 minutes, or until slightly thickened.

4   Meanwhile, bring a kettle of water to a boil. Pour into a saucepan, season with salt, and return to a boil. Add the pasta, then stir and cook for 10 minutes, or until al dente. Drain the pasta, reserving the water.

5   Add the pasta to the sauce and stir well to coat. Add a ladleful of the pasta water, if needed. Season to taste, then add the Parmesan and basil and stir again.

6   Serve in warm bowls and sprinkle with the reserved pancetta and a little more Parmesan.

Linguine Vongole with 'Nduja and Cherry Tomatoes

Serves 4

¾ cup dry white wine

3½ pounds clams, rinsed

3 tablespoons olive oil

2 shallots, peeled and finely diced

6 garlic cloves, peeled and finely sliced

3 ounces 'nduja sausage

8 ounces cherry tomatoes, halved

14 ounces linguine

2 small handfuls of flat-leaf parsley, finely chopped, plus extra to serve

Sea salt and freshly ground black pepper

'Nduja is a soft, spreadable salami from the Calabria region of Italy, and is seriously hot and spicy. It is usually spread on toast or served with cheese, but can also be stirred through pasta sauces, scrambled eggs, soups, and stews to add color and warmth. Shellfish, such as clams, love a bit of heat, but the sweetness of the tomatoes keeps this dish from being over the top.

1 Place a saucepan that has a tight-fitting lid over high heat until smoking hot. Meanwhile, line a colander with cheesecloth and sit it over another pan.

2 Pour the wine into the smoking pan, add the clams, then cover with the lid and cook for 3–4 minutes, until the clams have opened. Discard any that remain closed. Strain the rest through the prepared colander.

3 Place a large sauté pan over medium heat, add the olive oil and shallots, and cook for 2 minutes. Add the garlic and cook for an additional 2 minutes.

4 Increase the heat, add the 'nduja, and break it up with a spoon. Cook for another 2 minutes, then pour in the clam liquor and cook for 5 minutes before adding the tomatoes.

5 Bring a kettle of water to a boil, then pour it into a saucepan, season with salt, and return to a boil. Add the pasta and cook for 10 minutes, or until al dente.

6 While the sauce is simmering and the pasta is cooking, pick the meat from all but a dozen or so of the clams.

7 When the pasta is ready, drain in a colander, reserving the cooking water. Add the pasta to the sauce along with a ladleful of the reserved water, the clam meat, and the parsley. Toss the pan well in order to coat the pasta with the sauce.

8 Season to taste, then serve in warm bowls, garnished with the clams in their shells and some extra parsley.

Crab and Zucchini Spaghetti

Serves 4

7 ounces spaghetti

2 tablespoons olive oil

1 shallot, peeled and finely chopped

3 garlic cloves, peeled and thinly sliced

1 long red chile, seeded if you want a
   milder hit, finely chopped

¼ cup dry white wine

10 ounces zucchini, grated or julienned

7 ounces crab meat

½ cup crème fraîche

Zest of 1 lemon

2 tablespoons roughly chopped dill

3 tablespoons butter, cubed

Sea salt and freshly ground black
   pepper

Gone are the days when you would have to cook a live crab to make this pasta sauce; happily, you can now buy prepared crab meat from fishmongers and supermarkets, which saves you the bother. It is expensive because it can only be done by hand, but worth it to be able to cook this lovely, light summer dish in half an hour. Don't cook the crab for long or it will lose some of its gentle flavors.

1 Bring a kettle of water to a boil. Pour into a saucepan, season with salt, and return to a boil. Add the pasta and cook for 10 minutes, or until al dente.

2 Meanwhile, place a large nonstick sauté pan over medium-high heat and add the oil. When hot, add the shallot and cook for 2 minutes.

3 Add the garlic and chile and cook for an additional 2 minutes. Pour in the white wine, then increase the heat to high and cook until the wine reduces by half.

4 Add the zucchini, crab meat, and crème fraîche and stir well.

5 Drain the spaghetti, reserving the water. Add the pasta to the sauté pan along with half a ladleful of the cooking water, the lemon zest, half the dill, and the butter and cook for 1 minute. Toss the pasta to ensure it is well coated with the sauce and season to taste.

6 Serve in bowls, sprinkled with the remaining dill.

Farfalle with Brown Butter, Peas, and Sage

Serves 4

14 ounces farfalle

8 ounces fresh peas

3 ounces Parmesan cheese, grated, plus extra to serve

Sea salt and freshly ground black pepper

For the brown butter

14 tablespoons butter

Large handful of sage leaves

3 garlic cloves, peeled and finely chopped

Chef's tip

Get into the habit of always putting a bowl under the colander when draining pasta so you never pour the starchy cooking water down the plughole—you always need a little to help the sauce really stick to the pasta.

Despite being a really quick recipe, this is a deeply delicious pasta sauce. Browning, or burning, the butter completely transforms the flavor into something much richer and more interesting. Hold your nerve during the browning, and don't take the pan off the heat until you smell the telltale aroma—it should be sweet and nutty with rich caramel notes.

1 Bring a kettle of water to a boil. Half-fill a saucepan with it, season with salt, and return to a boil. (It's important to add just enough water to cover the pasta so that the water will become as starchy as possible.) Add the pasta, stir well, and cook for 10 minutes, or until al dente.

2 Meanwhile, put the butter into a sauté pan and place it over high heat. When it begins to brown, remove from the heat, add the sage leaves and garlic, and stir well.

3 Drain the pasta, reserving the cooking water.

4 Pour a ladleful of the reserved water into the sauté pan and add the peas. Return the pan to the heat and cook for 1–2 minutes, stirring constantly.

5 Add the pasta and Parmesan and stir well. Add a little more pasta water, if needed, and season to taste.

6 Serve in warm bowls with a twist of black pepper and extra Parmesan sprinkled on top.

Porcini Tagliatelle with Pine Nuts

Serves 2

½ ounce dried porcini mushrooms

7 ounces tagliatelle

¼ cup pine nuts

1 tablespoon olive oil

4 tablespoons butter

1 shallot, peeled and finely chopped

2 garlic cloves, peeled and finely
chopped

½ cup dry white wine

7 ounces fresh mushrooms, ideally
porcini or wild mushrooms, thinly
sliced

2 tablespoons finely chopped tarragon

1 ounce Parmesan cheese, finely
grated, plus extra to serve

1 tablespoon flat-leaf parsley, roughly
chopped

3 tablespoons crème fraîche

Sea salt and freshly ground black
pepper

You can use any variety of mushrooms for this sauce, as each type will bring something different to the finished dish. Try a wild mushroom mixture, or use fresh porcini when they are in season during the autumn. Always include the dried porcini, though—rehydrating them in boiling water creates an instant mushroom stock that is packed with flavor and gives the sauce a real boost.

1 Bring a kettle of water to a boil. Put the dried porcini into a small, heatproof bowl and add enough boiling water to cover them. Cover with plastic wrap and set aside.

2 Pour the remaining boiling water into a saucepan, add some salt, and return to a boil. Add the pasta and cook for 7–10 minutes, until al dente.

3 Meanwhile, put the pine nuts into a dry frying pan and place over medium heat, shaking the pan until they are lightly toasted. Set aside until needed.

4 Put the olive oil and half the butter into a sauté pan and place over low heat. When the butter has melted, add the shallot and cook gently for 2–3 minutes. Add the garlic and cook gently for another 2 minutes.

5 Increase the heat to high, add the white wine, and let it reduce by half.

6 Strain the liquid from the soaked porcini directly into the pan, then roughly chop the hydrated mushrooms and add them too. When the liquid has reduced by half, add the fresh mushrooms and tarragon and stir well until the mushrooms have softened.

7 Drain the pasta, reserving the water. Add the pasta to the mushroom mixture, then stir in the Parmesan, parsley, and remaining butter, plus some of the reserved water, if needed.

8 Season the pasta to taste, stir in the crème fraîche, and serve in bowls, sprinkled with extra Parmesan and the pine nuts.

Saffron Orzo with Turkey Meatballs

Serves 4

1 pound ground dark turkey meat

1½ ounces Parmesan cheese, finely
   grated, plus extra to serve

3 tablespoons flat-leaf parsley, finely
   chopped

Zest of 1 lemon

1 egg, lightly beaten

½ cup fresh breadcrumbs

½ cup all-purpose flour

1 tablespoon olive oil

1 cup chicken stock

Sea salt and freshly ground black
   pepper

For the saffron orzo

5½ tablespoons butter

2 shallots, peeled and finely diced

2 garlic cloves, peeled and finely
   chopped

Pinch of ground saffron

1 quart chicken stock

14 ounces orzo

2 tablespoons finely chopped oregano
   leaves

¾ ounce Parmesan cheese, finely
   grated

When you're keen to get dinner on the table in half an hour, risotto is out of the question; it simply takes too long for the rice to reach that ideal creamy texture. Orzo, however, cooks in 10 minutes and is equally velvety and comforting. When it comes to the meatballs, always buy ground dark turkey meat—it will be much more flavorful than the breast and juicier too.

1   Put the ground turkey, Parmesan, parsley, lemon zest, egg, and breadcrumbs into a large bowl and season with salt and pepper. Mix well and divide into 24 walnut-sized meatballs. Place in the fridge until needed.

2   To make the orzo, melt half the butter in a large sauté pan over medium heat. Add the shallots and cook for 2 minutes, then add the garlic and cook for an additional 2 minutes.

3   Add the saffron and quart of stock and bring to a boil. Pour in the orzo and cook for 10 minutes, or until al dente, stirring occasionally.

4   Remove the meatballs from the fridge and lightly coat each one in the flour. Place a large nonstick frying pan over high heat. When hot, pour in the olive oil, add the meatballs, and cook until golden brown all over.

5   Pour the 1 cup stock into the pan, bring to a simmer, and cook the meatballs gently for an additional 5 minutes, or until cooked through and the sauce has thickened.

6   When the orzo is ready, stir in the oregano, then add the Parmesan and remaining butter. Season to taste and serve in warm bowls with the turkey meatballs and some extra Parmesan on top.

Korean-Style Shrimp Fried Rice

Serves 4

2 eggs, lightly beaten
2 tablespoons vegetable oil
2 tablespoons sesame oil
14 ounces peeled raw jambo shrimp,
    cut in half lengthwise
2 tablespoons gochujang chile paste
3 (8.8-ounce) packets of microwavable
    long grain and wild rice, cooked
2 tablespoons soy sauce
1 tablespoon fish sauce
2 large handfuls of bean sprouts
1 cup frozen peas
Sea salt and ground white pepper

To serve

½ cup kimchi, roughly chopped
1 teaspoon black sesame seeds
Large handful of crispy fried onions
    (available from supermarkets)
4 spring onions, trimmed and thinly
    sliced at an angle
Sriracha sauce

If you have more time...

...and are feeling indulgent, fry
some eggs and place them on
top of the rice before garnishing.
The runny yolk seeping into the
rice is amazing.

The Korean gochujang chile paste stirred through this fried rice gives it a lovely color and a great kick, while the kimchi gives it the sour, fermented flavor that is associated with Korean food. Of course, fried rice is only a quick option if you have leftover or pre-cooked rice, as it has to be completely cold when stir-fried, or it will be soggy and disappointing.

1   Place a large nonstick wok over high heat. Season the eggs with salt and white pepper.
2   Add half of the two oils to the pan, swirl around to coat, then pour in the eggs. Cook for 1 minute, stirring gently to break them into pieces, then slide them onto a plate.
3   Return the wok to high heat. When hot, add the remaining oils, then the shrimp, and stir-fry for 1–2 minutes. Add the gochujang paste and stir well.
4   Add the rice, soy sauce, and fish sauce and stir-fry for another 2–3 minutes. Return the eggs to the pan, add the bean sprouts and peas, then stir-fry for an additional 2–3 minutes.
5   Serve the rice in warm bowls, garnished with the kimchi, sesame seeds, crispy fried onions, spring onions, and a drizzle of sriracha.

Chicken Biryani

Serves 4

2 tablespoons vegetable oil

1 onion, peeled and diced

1 large carrot, peeled and diced

2 garlic cloves, peeled and crushed

1-inch piece of fresh ginger, peeled
    and grated

2 tablespoons Madras curry paste

12 ounces boneless chicken thighs,
    cut into 3/4-inch cubes

2 ripe tomatoes, diced

2 cups basmati rice

3 cups chicken stock

2 large handfuls of baby spinach

2 large handfuls of fresh cilantro

¾ cup fresh or frozen peas

Sea salt and freshly ground black
    pepper

Papadums, to serve

For the minted yogurt

1½ teaspoons ground cumin

1¼ cups plain yogurt

Small handful of fresh mint,
    finely chopped

Biryani is a firm family favorite in our house, being mildly spiced but still full of flavor and nicely filling. In India, biryani is traditionally a layered dish, but this all-in-together version is quick, light, and just as tasty. We always make our own curry pastes in the restaurants, but a good-quality ready-made version is a speedy shortcut that won't compromise the end result in any way.

1   Place a large nonstick saucepan over medium-high heat and add the oil. When hot, add the onion and cook for 2–3 minutes. Add the carrot and cook for 2 minutes.

2   Stir in the garlic and ginger, then add the curry paste and cook for 1–2 minutes.

3   Add the chicken, stir well, then add the tomatoes, rice, and stock, and season with salt and pepper. Stir again and bring to a simmer. Cover and cook over low heat for 10 minutes.

4   Meanwhile, prepare the minted yogurt. Put the cumin into a small frying pan over high heat and stir until roasted and aromatic. Transfer to a small bowl, add the yogurt and mint, season with salt and pepper, and mix well.

5   Roughly chop the spinach and cilantro, then add them to the chicken pan together with the peas. Stir well and cook for an additional 2–3 minutes.

6   Serve the curry in bowls with the minted yogurt and papadums alongside.

Spanish Chorizo Rice

Serves 4

10 ounces spicy chorizo sausages

2 tablespoons olive oil

1 red onion, peeled and finely diced

1 large green pepper, seeded
and diced

2 garlic cloves, peeled and thinly sliced

1 teaspoon hot smoked paprika

1 teaspoon ground cumin

2 tablespoons tomato purée

7 ounces cherry tomatoes, halved

Pinch of ground saffron

1¼ cups chicken stock

7 ounces cooked piquillo peppers

3 (8.8-ounce) packages of
microwavable long-grain rice,
cooked

1 (14-ounce) can of black beans,
drained and rinsed

¾ cup pitted green olives

Sea salt and freshly ground black
pepper

To serve

Small handful of flat-leaf parsley,
roughly chopped

1 ounce Manchego cheese, shaved
(optional)

The paprika-flavored oil from the chorizo permeates this cracking rice dish, making it rich, sumptuous, and very moreish. When I don't have time to make an authentic paella from scratch, I cheat and use pre-cooked long-grain rice. This has a different texture from the short-grain Bomba rice traditionally used in paella, but it carries the flavors beautifully.

1 Place a large sauté pan over medium heat. Cut the chorizo into thick slices, then add to the pan with the olive oil. Cook for 5 minutes, or until browned and crispy on both sides. Transfer to a plate.

2 Add the onion to the pan and cook in the chorizo fat for 2–3 minutes, until softened. Add the green pepper and garlic and cook for 2 minutes.

3 Add the paprika, cumin, and tomato purée and stir for 1 minute. Add the tomatoes, saffron, and stock and bring to a simmer.

4 Cut the piquillo peppers into thick slices and add to the pan along with the rice, black beans, and olives. Cook for 4–5 minutes.

5 Season with salt and pepper and sprinkle with the parsley and Manchego (if using) before serving.

Lentil and Bulgur Tabbouleh with Broiled Feta

Serves 4

1¾ cups bulgur wheat

4 pieces of feta cheese, roughly 2 ounces each

1 tablespoon olive oil

9 ounces mini cucumbers, thickly sliced

2 celery stalks, finely chopped

1 red onion, peeled and finely diced

7 ounces cherry tomatoes, halved

2 large handfuls of mint, roughly chopped

3½ ounces flat-leaf parsley, roughly chopped

1 (14-ounce) can of cooked lentils

Sea salt and freshly ground black pepper

For the dressing

¼ cup extra virgin olive oil

3 tablespoons pomegranate molasses

2 tablespoons red wine vinegar

¼ teaspoon ground allspice

To serve

½ cup pomegranate seeds

Lemon wedges

When you grill feta, it doesn't melt—it just becomes softer and creamier with deliciously crisp edges. It's amazing with this lentil-filled tabbouleh, as the salty, tangy cheese is tempered by the sweet and sticky pomegranate molasses in the dressing. You can serve the salad on its own or as part of a big summer lunch, perhaps with the Blood Orange, Radicchio, and Fennel Salad on page 196 and the Warm Eggplant, Tomato, and Burrata salad on page 25.

1 Preheat the broiler. Line a baking sheet with a silicone mat.

2 Bring a kettle of water to a boil. Put the bulgur into a small saucepan, cover generously with the boiled water, then bring to a boil over high heat. Cook for 7–10 minutes, until the bulgur has softened.

3 Tip the cooked bulgur into a sieve and hold it under cold running water until cool. Drain well and set aside.

4 While the bulgur is cooking, place the feta on the prepared sheet, drizzle with the olive oil, and season with salt and pepper. Cook under the broiler for 10–12 minutes, until it has browned well.

5 Meanwhile, prepare all the vegetables and herbs as listed and put them into a large bowl with the lentils and bulgur.

6 Whisk together all the dressing ingredients, then pour over the bulgur mixture and stir well. Season to taste.

7 Remove the feta from the broiler and check that it is well colored. If any parts haven't browned properly, run a blowtorch over them, or return to the broiler for a few more minutes.

8 Divide the bulgur among four plates and place a piece of feta on top. Sprinkle with the pomegranate seeds and put a lemon wedge onto each plate before serving.

Crispy Chicken, Quinoa, and Cauliflower "Couscous" with Charred Corn

Serves 4

1 pound boneless chicken thighs, cut into strips ½ inch thick
2 tablespoons chipotle paste
1 teaspoon dried oregano
Vegetable oil, for frying
⅓ cup all-purpose flour
⅓ cup cornstarch
Sea salt and freshly ground black pepper
Lime wedges, to serve

For the quinoa and cauliflower "couscous"

2 ears corn on the cob
2 tablespoons olive oil
1 red onion, peeled and diced
12 ounces cauliflower, grated
9 ounces broccoli, finely chopped (including stems)
1½ cups cooked quinoa
5 ounces roasted red peppers, from a jar, thickly sliced
1 (14-ounce) can of kidney beans, drained and rinsed
2 large handfuls of fresh cilantro, roughly chopped
3 Little Gem lettuces, shredded

For the dressing

¼ cup extra virgin olive oil
2 teaspoons grainy mustard
1 tablespoon agave syrup
Juice of 2 limes

Time-saving tip

You can buy prepared cauliflower rice from the supermarket.

This brilliant, colorful salad is great with the crispy chicken, but would be equally good with fried smoked tofu, or grilled halloumi or feta. It's packed with superfoods, such as quinoa, kidney beans, and raw broccoli, so it's extremely good for you, as well as being very tasty and satisfying. Make double the batch and feel virtuous as you take it to work for lunch the next day.

1 Put the chicken, chipotle paste, and oregano into a bowl. Season with salt and pepper and mix well.

2 For the "couscous," remove the corn kernels from the cobs by standing each cob upright and running a sharp knife down the sides.

3 Place a large frying pan over high heat and add the olive oil. When hot, fry the corn until lightly charred.

4 Add the onion and cook for 1–2 minutes. Add the cauliflower and cook for an additional 2–3 minutes.

5 Remove the pan from the heat and stir in the broccoli, quinoa, red peppers, kidney beans, cilantro, and shredded lettuce. Transfer to a bowl and set aside.

6 Place a shallow sauté pan over high heat and add a ½-inch depth of oil. Combine the flour and cornstarch in a bowl, then lightly coat each piece of chicken in the mixture. Add to the hot oil in batches and cook until crisp outside with no sign of pink inside. When ready, drain on paper towels.

7 Meanwhile, whisk together the dressing ingredients and season with salt and pepper. Pour over the "couscous" and mix well. Spoon onto plates, top with the crispy fried chicken, and serve with wedges of lime.

Dips
and
Sides

Pea and Mint Guacamole

Serves 4

1¼ cups frozen peas
1 tablespoon olive oil
1 small onion, peeled and thinly
  sliced
2 ripe avocados
Juice of 2 limes
3 mint sprigs, leaves picked
Sea salt and freshly ground black
  pepper

Time-saving tip

To peel avocados quickly and
with minimal waste, cut them
in half around the pit, then
slip a spoon between the flesh
and the skin and run it gently
around the fruit, keeping the
back of the spoon as close to
the skin as possible. The flesh
should pop out easily, leaving
very little behind.

This dip is seriously green! It's so much brighter, fresher, and better for you than store-bought guacamole, and is really quick and simple to make. It's a great standby recipe too, as chances are that you already have all the ingredients in the kitchen. It is great with crunchy vegetables, such as radishes, baby carrots, sugarsnap peas, Little Gem lettuce leaves, and mini cucumbers, but also with tortilla chips or spread on toast as an alternative to hummus.

1 Put the peas into a colander and hold under running tepid water for about a minute to defrost them.
2 Place a frying pan over medium heat and add the oil. When hot, sweat the onion for 3–4 minutes, until soft, stirring regularly to keep it from sticking.
3 Slice the avocados in half, remove the pits, and scoop out the flesh with a spoon. Chop the flesh and put it into a blender or bowl with the lime juice and mint leaves.
4 Add the peas to the onions in the frying pan and allow to warm through for a minute.
5 Tip the onions and peas into the blender or bowl and season with salt and pepper. Pulse or mash with a fork just until the mixture combines—you want to retain some texture. Taste and adjust the seasoning as necessary. Serve with a selection of crunchy vegetables or chips.

Black Hummus with Pita Chips

Serves 4

4 pita breads

½ cup olive oil, plus extra for
drizzling

1 (14-ounce) can of chickpeas, drained
and rinsed

⅓ cup black sesame paste

1 garlic clove, peeled and crushed

1 rosemary sprig, leaves finely
chopped

Juice of 1–2 lemons

Sea salt

Swapping regular tahini for black sesame paste in this hummus transforms the color but also subtly changes the taste, as black sesame seeds are less sweet than the lighter, cream-colored ones, and have an earthy nuttiness that goes brilliantly with the rosemary and garlic in this dip. Black sesame paste can be found in Asian supermarkets, as it's a staple in Japanese cooking, where they often sweeten it with honey and use it in pastries and ice cream. However, it's also really delicious just spread on toast.

1 Preheat the oven to 400°F.

2 Cut each pita bread into 8 triangles. Split open each triangle and separate the halves, removing any bready dough that is attached. Arrange the triangles in a single layer on two baking sheets, then drizzle with olive oil and sprinkle with sea salt before placing in the oven for 3–4 minutes.

3 Put the chickpeas, sesame paste, garlic, rosemary, 2 tablespoons olive oil, and the juice from 1 lemon into a food processor. Season with salt and blend until you have a smooth paste. Taste the hummus and add more olive oil, lemon juice, and salt as necessary.

4 Take the pita chips out of the oven and turn them over, removing the thinner ones that have already crisped up. Return the sheets to the oven for another 2–3 minutes, until all the remaining triangles are golden brown and crunchy.

5 Transfer the hummus to a bowl and drizzle with a little olive oil before serving with the pita chips.

Anchovy Tapenade with Ciabatta Toasts

Serves 4–6

½ ciabatta loaf

3–4 tablespoons olive oil, plus extra for drizzling

2 (1.5-ounce) jars of good-quality anchovies in olive oil

2 garlic cloves, peeled and crushed

1 shallot, peeled and finely diced

Small handful of parsley leaves

1 cup pitted Kalamata olives

2 teaspoons red wine vinegar

Sea salt and freshly ground black pepper

Take two classics of Mediterranean cooking, anchovies and olives, blitz them together with a good-quality extra virgin olive oil, and you have a punchy dip or an intense topping for bruschetta in under 20 minutes. Serve with crunchy veg or lightly toasted bread and a chilled bottle of white wine and be instantly transported to a terrace in the South of France.

1 Preheat the broiler to high.

2 Slice the ciabatta very thinly into 8–10 slices, then drizzle with olive oil on each side and lay them on a baking sheet. Place under the broiler and toast for 2–3 minutes on each side, until golden brown and crisp. Beware—the thinner the bread, the quicker it will burn, so check often.

3 Meanwhile, drain the anchovies, reserving any oil. Put the fish into a food processor with the garlic, shallot, parsley, and olives and blitz to a purée.

4 Add the red wine vinegar and season with salt and pepper, then, with the motor running, pour in any reserved anchovy oil, followed by the measured olive oil until you reach the desired consistency.

5 Taste and adjust the seasoning as necessary, then serve with the crisp ciabatta toasts and crudités.

Blood Orange, Radicchio, and Fennel Salad

Serves 4

1 fennel bulb
3 blood oranges
1 head of radicchio, or a mixture
 of different varieties, such as
 Trevisano or Castelfranco

For the dressing
3 tablespoons white balsamic vinegar
1 teaspoon honey
1 teaspoon grainy mustard
Juice of ½ blood orange
Juice of ½ lemon
2 tablespoons chopped dill
¼ cup extra virgin olive oil
Sea salt and freshly ground black
 pepper

Try to get your hands on a few different varieties of radicchio for this salad, such as the pale, red-splattered leaves of Castelfranco, the curly fingers of Trevisano Tardivo, or the classic Chioggia, to make it even more of a visual feast. It looks stunning with the blood oranges and sliced fennel, and makes a beautiful addition to a big lunch. Serve with chicken, fish, or grilled meats, or turn it into a starter by placing a couple of burratas on top. If you can't get radicchio, red chicory will work just as well flavor-wise.

1 Trim the fennel, cut it into quarters, then slice it very thinly using a mandoline.

2 Using a sharp knife, peel the oranges, being careful to remove all the pith. Thinly slice the flesh into discs.

3 Remove the core from the radicchio and tear the leaves into bite-sized pieces. Put these into a large salad bowl and add the fennel and blood orange slices.

4 Combine all the dressing ingredients in a bowl, season with salt and pepper, and whisk well. Taste and, if necessary, add more acidity or sweetness.

5 Pour half the dressing into the salad bowl and mix carefully with your hands until everything is coated. Drizzle the remaining dressing over the top before serving.

Moroccan Carrot Salad

Serves 4

1 pound carrots
2 tablespoons rose harissa
1 tablespoon finely chopped preserved
   lemon
1 green chile, seeded and thinly
   sliced
2 garlic cloves, peeled and crushed
Juice of 1 lemon
1 teaspoon ground cumin
2 tablespoons olive oil
Large handful of cilantro leaves,
   roughly chopped
Sea salt and freshly ground black
   pepper

Time-saving tip

To save more time, don't peel the carrots—a lot of the goodness is just under the skin and gets lost by peeling, so give them a brisk scrub instead.

I recently visited Morocco to film a TV show, and I fell in love with all the North African flavors, including harissa, preserved lemon, cinnamon, cumin, and rose water. This stunning dressing works brilliantly with other ingredients too, so make a double batch and keep it in the fridge to drizzle over some grilled halloumi or roasted cauliflower, or to stir through a big bowl of couscous. Alternatively, drizzle some extra olive oil over the top and serve it as a dip with flatbreads and baby veg.

1 Bring a kettle of water to a boil, then pour it into a saucepan and place over medium heat.
2 Peel the carrots and cut them into thin rounds. Add them to the boiling water, bring to a boil again, then drain immediately. Transfer the carrots to a bowl of iced water to stop them from cooking.
3 Meanwhile, put the harissa, preserved lemon, chile, garlic, lemon juice, cumin, and olive oil into a small saucepan and place it over medium heat for 2–3 minutes to warm through and combine.
4 Drain the carrots thoroughly and transfer them to a serving dish. Spoon over the dressing and stir well. Season with salt and pepper, then sprinkle with the chopped cilantro and stir again before serving.

Green Beans with Tarragon and Pine Nuts

Serves 4

¼ cup pine nuts

12 ounces green beans

2 tablespoons butter

2–3 tarragon sprigs, leaves roughly
  chopped

Sea salt

Time-saving tip

Toast more pine nuts than you
need and keep the excess in an
airtight jar to speed things up
next time you need to scatter
them over a salad or pasta dish,
such as Porcini Tagliatelle (see
page 172).

This is a great way to make green beans more
interesting without having to do very much. Suddenly
a boring side dish has a bit more to say for itself!
It makes a cracking accompaniment to grilled fish,
roast chicken, and grilled lamb or pork chops,
or you could swap the butter for a light vinaigrette
and serve it as a salad as part of a summer lunch.

1 Bring a kettle of water to a boil, then pour it into a
   saucepan and bring to a boil with the lid on.
2 Place a small frying pan over medium heat and add
   the pine nuts in a single layer. Toast for about 4 minutes,
   shaking the pan from time to time, particularly toward
   the end of the cooking time.
3 Add the green beans to the boiling water and cook for
   5 minutes, or until cooked but still crisp.
4 Drain the beans and return them to the empty pan.
   Add the butter and, with the lid on, shake the pan a
   couple of times until the butter has melted and coated
   the beans.
5 Tip the beans into a serving dish, mix in the tarragon
   leaves, and sprinkle over the toasted pine nuts. Season
   with salt before serving.

Zucchini Fries

Serves 4

3 medium zucchinis
Pinch of saffron
½ cup water
1 quart neutral oil, such as peanut,
   for frying
1 cup semolina
½ cup all-purpose flour
Sea salt
Dried marjoram, to serve

Chef's tip

If you don't have a cooking
thermometer, the oil is ready
(350°F) when a cube of bread
added to it browns in 30 seconds.

We serve these crispy zucchini fries in Union Street Café in London, where they are hugely popular with people just ordering a drink after work. They also go really well with burgers (see pages 105 and 135), grilled chicken, and fish. Alternatively, just scatter some crumbled feta over the fries to make a meal of them. Be warned—they are very moreish!

1 Finely julienne the zucchini with a mandoline or julienne peeler and put them into a large bowl.
2 Season the zucchini with plenty of salt to release the water.
3 Using a mortar and pestle, grind the saffron to a powder and sprinkle it over the zucchini. Add the water, stir well, and set aside for 10–15 minutes.
4 Meanwhile, pour the oil into a large heavy-based saucepan and place over medium-high heat.
5 Mix the semolina and all-purpose flour together in a large bowl.
6 Once the oil has reached 350°F, lift a handful of the zucchini from the water and toss them in the flour mixture until lightly coated. Fry them in the hot oil until golden and crisp. Using a slotted spoon, transfer them to a plate lined with paper towels. Repeat this step with the remaining zucchini.
7 Transfer the fries to a serving bowl and season with salt and the marjoram before serving.

Aromatic Saffron Pilaf

Serves 4

3½ tablespoons ghee or butter
1 large onion, thinly sliced
2 cups basmati rice
Pinch of saffron
Small handful of curry leaves
3½ cups chicken stock
1 cinnamon stick
5 cardamom pods
5 cloves
1 teaspoon sea salt

A spiced pilaf is such a versatile dish and makes a great addition to curry night. Try it with the Malaysian Fish and Okra Curry on page 53, or the Ground Lamb Curry on page 117. Get all the prep done up front and you won't have to worry about time—you can just get on with cooking the main event. It will make your kitchen smell heavenly in the meantime.

1   Place a nonstick saucepan over high heat and add the ghee (or butter). When hot, add the onion and cook for 5–8 minutes, stirring occasionally.

2   Meanwhile, put the rice into a large bowl and cover with water. Swirl it around with your hand, then pour out the water. Refill the bowl and repeat until the water is clear. Drain and set aside.

3   Using a mortar and pestle, grind the saffron to a powder.

4   Add the curry leaves to the onion and cook for 1 minute. Now add the saffron, chicken stock, cinnamon stick, cardamom pods, cloves, salt, and rice. Stir well and cover with a lid. Bring to a boil, then immediately reduce the heat to low. Allow to cook for 12–15 minutes, then turn the heat off and leave to sit for 2–3 minutes before serving.

Decadent Mashed Potatoes with Three Variations

Serves 4

2 pounds Yukon Gold potatoes,
    peeled and cut into ½-inch cubes
5½ tablespoons butter
½ cup whole milk
½ cup heavy cream
Sea salt and freshly ground black
    pepper

Variation 1: Mustard Mash

1 teaspoon English mustard
1 tablespoon Dijon mustard
2 teaspoons grainy mustard

Variation 2: Truffle Mash

2 tablespoons porcini and truffle paste
2 tablespoons white truffle oil

Variation 3: Garlic and Herb Mash

2 garlic cloves, peeled and crushed
2 tablespoons finely chopped woody
    herbs, e.g., rosemary, thyme, sage
2 tablespoons finely chopped soft
    herbs, e.g., parsley, chives, dill

Chef's tip

The hotter the potato when you put it through the ricer, the fluffier the mash, so move fast once the potatoes have been drained.

Mashed potatoes are a great accompaniment for so many dishes, but these three decadent options are almost worthy of top billing. Pair them with a rib eye steak, some good-quality sausages, or a robust fillet of whitefish and you have simple, fast food without any fuss. Investing in a potato ricer will make mashing the potatoes much easier and quicker, and the results are so much smoother than with a conventional masher. Once you've tried one, you'll never look back.

1   Bring a pan of salted water to a boil. Add the potatoes and cook for 15 minutes with the lid on.

2   Meanwhile, if you're making the regular, mustard, or truffle mash, put the butter, milk, and cream into a small saucepan and bring to a gentle simmer. For the mustard mash, add the mustards to the warm cream mixture. For the truffle mash, add the truffle paste and truffle oil to the pan instead.

3   For the garlic and herb mash, heat the butter in a small saucepan, add the garlic and woody herbs, and cook for 2–3 minutes. Pour in the milk and cream and bring to a gentle simmer. Add the soft herbs and cook for another 2–3 minutes.

4   When the potatoes are cooked, drain in a colander. Put them through a potato ricer as quickly as possible and return them to the saucepan.

5   Pour over the flavored cream and mix well. Season to taste with salt and pepper, stir again, and serve.

Desserts

Burnt Meringue with Poached Rhubarb

Serves 4

12 ounces rhubarb, cut into 2-inch
  lengths
2 tablespoons grenadine liqueur
Zest and juice of ½ orange
Seeds from 1 vanilla pod
¼ cup superfine sugar
2 tablespoons water
5 ounces strawberries, thickly sliced
Crème fraîche, to serve

For the pistachio crumble
2 tablespoons butter
¼ cup all-purpose flour
¼ cup superfine sugar
¼ cup shelled pistachios

For the meringue
3 large egg whites
½ cup superfine sugar

The secret to perfect, crisp meringues is cooking them at a low temperature really, really slowly, which rules them out for this book. However, the soft meringues here are cooked at the last minute with a blowtorch, bringing a lovely dark caramel flavor to the finished dish. The result is a restaurant-quality dessert that is still produced within 30 minutes.

1 Preheat the oven to 350°F. Line a small baking sheet with parchment paper.
2 Start by making the pistachio crumble: put the butter, flour, and sugar into a food processor and pulse until the mixture resembles breadcrumbs. Add the pistachios and pulse just a couple of times, until the nuts are roughly chopped. Pour the mixture onto the prepared sheet and place in the oven for 10–15 minutes, until lightly golden.
3 Meanwhile, put the rhubarb into a small saucepan with the grenadine, orange zest and juice, vanilla seeds, sugar, and water. Place over high heat, cover with a lid, and cook for 3–4 minutes, until the rhubarb is tender but still holding its shape. Using a slotted spoon, transfer the rhubarb to a bowl.
4 Return the pan to the stovetop and simmer the liquid until it reduces to a medium-thick syrup. Leave to cool slightly, then fold in the strawberries, followed by the rhubarb.
5 Remove the crumble from the oven and leave to cool.
6 To make the meringue, put the egg whites into a large bowl and beat with a handheld electric mixer until soft peaks form. Gradually add the sugar, 2 tablespoons at a time, until it is all incorporated and firm peaks have formed.
7 Smear a spoonful of the meringue onto each plate. Place the remainder in a piping bag and pipe a few meringue "kisses" on each plate. Run a blowtorch over the meringue until golden and burnt in places.
8 Spoon some rhubarb mixture onto each plate. Drizzle over the syrup, then add a spoonful of crème fraîche. Finally, break up the pistachio crumble and sprinkle over the top before serving.

Mango, White Chocolate, and Passion Fruit Parfaits

Serves 4

⅓ cup coconut flakes
9 ounces ripe mango flesh
⅓ cup passion fruit pulp
(about 2 fruits)
Zest of ½ lime
Juice of 1 lime

For the mousse

⅓ cup coconut milk
2½ cups mini marshmallows
1 cup white chocolate chips
1 cup heavy cream
1 teaspoon vanilla paste
1 cup passion fruit pulp
(about 5–6 fruits)

Time-saving tip

Make sure you create space in your freezer before you start, as you will need it for chilling the white chocolate and the mousse.

Time-saving tip

If you can't find fresh passion fruit, many grocers sell passion fruit pulp.

When time is short, it is difficult to produce a fancy layered dessert with lots of different elements, as you have to wait for each layer to set before adding another. A parfait in a glass or bowl, however, is a great way to pull it off, and this white chocolate version with mango, passion fruit, and coconut is exquisite.

1 Place four serving glasses in the freezer to chill.
2 To make the mousse, put the coconut milk and marshmallows into a small saucepan, place over medium heat, and stir until the marshmallows have melted, 2–3 minutes. Place the white chocolate in a small heatproof bowl, pour in the marshmallow mixture, and stir until the chocolate has melted. Pour this mixture into a shallow tray and put straight into the freezer to cool down quickly.
3 Whip the cream and vanilla paste with an electric mixer until stiff peaks form, 2–3 minutes. Fold the 1 cup passion fruit pulp into the cream.
4 Remove the white chocolate from the freezer and make sure it's cool. Transfer to a mixing bowl, add a spoonful of the cream, and whisk until well combined. Gently fold in the rest of the cream until combined.
5 Remove the glasses from the freezer and spoon the mousse into them. Return them to the freezer for 10 minutes.
6 Meanwhile, toast the coconut flakes in a small frying pan over medium-high heat, 2–3 minutes, until golden brown, shaking the pan often. Set aside to cool.
7 Chop the mango into ½-inch dice and mix with the passion fruit pulp and lime zest and juice.
8 Spoon the mango mixture into the glasses and sprinkle with the toasted coconut before serving.

Spiced Peach, Apple, and Almond Crumble

Serves 6

2 (15-ounce) cans peach slices, drained

1 pound peeled and diced apple (about 3 fruits)

3 tablespoons marmalade

1 teaspoon pumpkin pie spice

¼ cup light brown sugar

3½ ounces soft amaretti cookies, crumbled

½ cup orange juice

¼ cup almond liqueur

Whipped cream, crème fraîche, or ice cream, to serve

For the almond crumble

¾ cup flour

7 tablespoons cold butter, diced

½ cup superfine sugar

1 teaspoon almond extract

⅓ cup sliced almonds, roughly chopped

½ cup rolled oats

Chef's tip

Make this crumble in advance, then put it into the oven when you sit down to your main course. It will be bubbling and golden brown by the time you are ready for dessert.

Using good-quality canned peaches means not only that you avoid having to prep any fresh fruit, but also that you can enjoy this fragrant spiced crumble all year round. The combination of sweet peaches, tart apples, and distinct almond flavor is a knockout, and certain to be a crowd pleaser whatever time of year you rustle it up.

1　Preheat the oven to 400°F.

2　Place the peaches, apple, marmalade, and pumpkin pie spice in a medium bowl. Mix well and spread in a shallow, ovenproof, 2-quart dish. Sprinkle over the brown sugar and amaretti, then pour in the orange juice and almond liqueur.

3　To make the crumble, put the flour, butter, and superfine sugar into a medium bowl and quickly rub together until the mixture resembles breadcrumbs. Add the remaining ingredients and mix well. Sprinkle the crumble over the fruit.

4　Place the dish on the top shelf of the oven for 25–30 minutes, until the apples are tender and the crumble topping is golden brown.

5　Serve with unsweetened whipped cream, crème fraîche, or ice cream.

Pain Perdu with Summer Fruit Compote

Serves 4

1 (14-ounce) unsliced brioche loaf

2 large eggs

½ cup whole milk

½ cup heavy cream

Seeds from 1 vanilla pod

½ teaspoon ground cinnamon

½ teaspoon ground cardamom

2 tablespoons superfine sugar, plus
   extra for sprinkling

1 tablespoon vegetable oil

4 tablespoons butter

Crème fraîche, to serve

For the compote

2 tablespoons crème de cassis liqueur

⅓ cup superfine sugar

6 ounces strawberries, thickly sliced

3½ ounces raspberries

3½ ounces blueberries

Chef's tip

The pain perdu can also be
served with the Winter Fruit
Compote on page 229,
depending on the time of year
and what fruits are in season.

Pain perdu is basically posh eggy bread, and this
lightly spiced version is made even more elegant by
being served with a simple compote of summer fruits.
If possible, use slightly old brioche for this, as it absorbs
more of the egg and cream mixture, and the finished
result will be crispier round the edges. You will need
a blowtorch to caramelize the sugar at the end, but if
you don't have one, simply dust the whole dish with
confectioners' sugar for a little extra sophistication.

1   Cut the brioche into large slices, about 4 x 2 inches,
    trimming off any excess crust.

2   Put the eggs into a bowl with the milk, cream, vanilla
    seeds, cinnamon, cardamom, and sugar and whisk
    together. Pour into a shallow dish.

3   Put the crème de cassis and sugar for the compote into
    a small saucepan over high heat and reduce to a
    medium-thick syrup, 2–3 minutes. Set aside.

4   Meanwhile, dip the brioche slices in the egg mixture
    for just 30 seconds each, turning them so that all
    sides are evenly coated.

5   Put the vegetable oil and butter into a large nonstick
    frying pan over medium-high heat. When the butter has
    melted, carefully add the brioche slices and cook until
    golden brown on both sides, 2–3 minutes per side.

6   Add the berries to the syrup and stir together gently.

7   Sprinkle a layer of sugar evenly on the presentation side
    of each brioche piece, then run a blowtorch over it until
    the sugar melts and turns golden brown.

8   To serve, place a slice of brioche on each plate, adding
    a spoonful of the compote and a dollop of crème fraîche
    on the side.

Banana Split with Salted Caramel Chocolate Sauce

Serves 2

⅓ cup pecans or macadamia nuts,
  or a mixture of both
1 tablespoon superfine sugar
2 ripe bananas, peeled and halved
  lengthwise
4 scoops of vanilla ice cream,
  to serve

For the sauce
⅓ cup dark brown sugar
1½ tablespoons butter
⅓ cup heavy cream
¼ cup dark chocolate chips
½ teaspoon sea salt

My kids love an old-school banana split, which has to be one of the quickest ever desserts to put together. This salted caramel version is not tricky or too time-consuming, but it takes this kids' favorite to a new level. Caramelizing the bananas brings out all the sophisticated flavors of vanilla, honey, and rum in the fruit, while the salted caramel in the chocolate sauce keeps the whole dish from being too sweet.

1 Preheat the oven to 400°F.
2 Start by making the sauce: put the brown sugar, butter, cream, and salt into a small saucepan and place over medium heat. Stir well and bring to a gentle simmer, then cook for 1 minute. Leave to cool for 1 minute.
3 Place the chocolate chips in a small heatproof bowl and pour the caramel over them. Stir until the chocolate has melted and the sauce is well combined, then leave to cool.
4 Put the nuts on a baking sheet and place in the oven for 5 minutes, or until lightly toasted. Allow to cool before roughly chopping them.
5 Sprinkle the superfine sugar over the cut sides of the bananas, then run a blowtorch over each one to caramelize it well. Alternatively, place the bananas, sugar side up, under a hot broiler for 5 minutes, or until caramelized.
6 Place two halves of banana on each serving plate, then put 2 scoops of ice cream in the middle. Drizzle the caramel sauce over the top and sprinkle with the toasted nuts before serving.

Cheat's Cheesecake with Macerated Strawberries

Serves 4

¾ cup (6 ounces) cream cheese
3 tablespoons confectioners' sugar
Squeeze of lemon juice
Seeds from ½ vanilla pod
1¼ cups heavy cream
4 full sheets graham crackers
3 tablespoons superfine sugar
3½ tablespoons unsalted butter
1 tablespoon mint leaves, to garnish

For the macerated strawberries

7 ounces strawberries, quartered
2 tablespoons confectioners' sugar
½ cup Sauternes, Muscat, or other
    sweet wine

Chef's tip

If you are feeding children, leave
out the sweet wine, or replace
it with lemon juice or balsamic
vinegar for a little added
sharpness.

Everyone loves a cheesecake, but the baking of the base and the setting of the cream cheese mean that it isn't the quickest dessert to whip up. This upside-down version, however, has all the elements of a traditional cheesecake, but with no hanging around. Macerating strawberries, which involves just sprinkling them with sugar and setting them aside, is a brilliant chef's trick for bringing out the sweetness in the fruit; it takes seconds to do, but the results are incredible.

1 Line four 7-ounce ramekins with plastic wrap and place them in the freezer to chill.
2 To macerate the strawberries, put them into a bowl with the confectioners' sugar and wine. Stir well, then cover with plastic wrap and set aside for 15–20 minutes.
3 Put the cream cheese and confectioners' sugar into a medium bowl. Add the lemon juice and vanilla seeds and mix together until smooth.
4 Pour the cream into a second bowl and whisk into soft peaks, then fold it into the cream cheese mixture.
5 Remove the chilled ramekins from the freezer and fill with the cream cheese mixture, levelling the surface with a palette knife or spatula. Place in the fridge until needed.
6 Put the graham crackers into a food processor and pulse into coarse crumbs. Alternatively, place them in a plastic bag and crush with a rolling pin.
7 Place a medium nonstick sauté pan over medium heat and add the superfine sugar. Once it has melted and begun to caramelize, carefully add the butter and gently shake the pan to combine it with the caramel as it melts.
8 Add the graham cracker crumbs and shake the pan to coat them in the caramel. Pour the mixture onto a plate and place in the fridge for 5 minutes. When cool, crumble into pieces.
9 Remove the ramekins from the fridge and turn out the cheesecakes onto plates, discarding the plastic wrap. Spoon the strawberries over and around the cheesecakes and sprinkle the graham cracker "base" over the top. Garnish with a little fresh mint before serving.

Fig Tarts with Vanilla and Honey Mascarpone

Serves 4

1 (14-ounce) sheet of frozen all-butter
   puff pastry, defrosted
6 ripe figs, thickly sliced
¼ teaspoon ground cinnamon
1 egg, lightly beaten
1 tablespoon brown sugar

For the vanilla and honey mascarpone

5 ounces mascarpone cheese
2 tablespoons honey, plus extra for
   drizzling
Seeds from 1 vanilla pod
Zest of ½ lemon

These tarts are so quick and easy to make that you really have no excuse for buying in dessert. Ripe figs with cinnamon is a gorgeous combination, but you can try this recipe with most fruits as they come into season—strawberries, blueberries, mango, and blackberries would all be delicious. The vanilla and honey mascarpone is an irresistible addition, but vanilla ice cream or crème fraîche would also be good if time is tight.

1   Preheat the oven to 425°F. Line a baking sheet with parchment paper.

2   Unroll the pastry and remove a strip about 1½ inches wide from each side (you can freeze these pieces for decorating future pies). Cut the remaining pastry into 4 equal rectangles. Place them on the prepared sheet, spacing them apart, then prick all over with a fork, leaving a ½-inch border around the edge.

3   Arrange the fig slices on top, slightly overlapping them in places, but keeping them inside the borders.

4   Sprinkle the cinnamon over the figs and brush the borders with the beaten egg. Sprinkle the entire surface of the tarts with the sugar, then place in the oven on a high shelf for 12–15 minutes, until the pastry is golden and crisp.

5   Meanwhile, place all the mascarpone ingredients in a small bowl and whisk together until smooth.

6   Remove the tarts from the oven and transfer to plates. Place a spoonful of the mascarpone beside each tart, then drizzle with a little extra honey before serving.

Rhubarb and Ginger Cheesecake Pots

Serves 4

10 ounces rhubarb, trimmed and cut
   into ¾-inch pieces
1 ounce crystallized ginger, finely
   chopped
2 tablespoons ginger syrup
2 tablespoons grenadine liqueur
2 tablespoons superfine sugar
4 ounces gingersnaps

For the cheesecake mixture
¾ cup heavy cream
¾ cup cream cheese, at room
   temperature
¾ cup Greek yogurt
Zest of ½ lemon
1 tablespoon vanilla extract
5 tablespoons superfine sugar
2 tablespoons orange liqueur

Here is another way to make a quick cheesecake (see page 222 for an upside-down version with macerated strawberries). It has a no-bake gingersnap base and is made in individual glasses, so the cream cheese layer doesn't need to set before serving. You can eat it as soon as you make it, or keep it in the fridge until needed.

1 Put the rhubarb, crystallized ginger, ginger syrup, grenadine, and sugar into a saucepan. Place over medium heat and cook for 4–5 minutes, stirring occasionally, until the rhubarb begins to soften around the edges. Pour the mixture into a shallow tray and place in the fridge to cool.

2 To make the cheesecake mixture, pour the cream into a bowl and whisk until soft peaks form. Place the remaining cheesecake ingredients in a separate bowl and whisk until combined. Fold in the cream.

3 Put the gingersnaps in a food processor and pulse into fine crumbs. Alternatively, place them in a plastic bag and crush with a rolling pin.

4 Divide the crumbs among four shallow serving glasses, then spoon in the cheesecake filling.

5 Remove the rhubarb topping from the fridge and spoon it into the glasses. Serve immediately, or cover and keep in the fridge until needed.

Cinnamon Ice Cream Sandwiches with Winter Fruit Compote

Serves 4

1 (14-ounce) sheet of frozen all-butter
   puff pastry, defrosted
2 tablespoons light brown sugar
2 teaspoons ground cinnamon
3 tablespoons butter, softened
4 large scoops of vanilla ice cream, to
   serve

For the compote

3½ ounces peeled and diced Granny
   Smith apple (about 1 fruit)
3½ ounces peeled and diced pear
   (about 1 fruit)
½ cup light brown sugar
½ cup red wine
½ teaspoon pumpkin pie spice
Zest and juice of ½ orange
3 ounces blackberries

Here is a clever way to transform a scoop of vanilla ice cream into something much more impressive with very little effort. The cinnamon pastry discs add spice and crunch, while the apple and blackberry compote provides a warming and sharp contrast. You can make the discs and the compote in advance, so it's just a case of putting all the elements together at the last minute.

1 Preheat the oven to 425°F. Line a baking sheet with parchment paper.

2 Cut the pastry in half lengthwise so that you end up with two 5 x 14-inch rectangles. Place one rectangle on the prepared sheet and place the other in the freezer for future use in another recipe.

3 Combine the brown sugar and cinnamon in a small bowl. Spread the butter evenly over the chilled pastry. Sprinkle the cinnamon sugar all over the butter and pat with a spoon to make sure it's well stuck down. With the narrower edge toward you, roll up the pastry tightly to form a thick roll, then place it in the freezer for 5 minutes to firm up.

4 Meanwhile, put all the compote ingredients, apart from the blackberries, into a small saucepan. Place over high heat and cook for 4–5 minutes.

5 Remove the cinnamon roll from the freezer and cut it into 8 slices about ½ inch thick. Line the backs of two baking sheets with parchment paper and place 4 slices of cinnamon roll on each sheet, spacing them well apart. Pat each one down lightly with your fingers, to about ¼-inch thick. Place a sheet of parchment paper over each sheet of rolls, then sit another baking sheet on top to weigh them down lightly. Place in the oven for 10 minutes. (If you don't have four baking sheets, bake the rolls in batches.)

6 Add the blackberries to the compote and cook for another 2–3 minutes. Set aside to cool slightly.

7 Remove the rolls from the oven and lift off the top sheets and paper. Set aside to cool.

8 When you are ready to serve, place a cinnamon roll on each plate. Top with a scoop of ice cream and place another cinnamon roll on top. Serve with a big spoonful of warm compote on the side.

Calvados Candy Apple Pancakes

Serves 4

¼ cup pecans
12 ounces green apples
7 tablespoons butter
¼ cup Calvados
½ teaspoon vanilla paste
½ cup dark brown sugar
½ cup heavy cream
Vanilla ice cream, to serve

For the pancake batter

1¼ cups all-purpose flour
1½ teaspoons baking powder
2 tablespoons superfine sugar
1 large egg
⅔ cup whole milk
2 tablespoons butter, melted
Pinch of salt

As children, we all love candy apples, but when was the last time you ate one as an adult? Inspired by this nostalgic flavor combination, these apples in caramel have been given a grown-up makeover by adding a touch of Calvados, or apple brandy, to the caramel, making it a little bit more sophisticated and utterly delicious.

1 Preheat the oven to 400°F.

2 Put the pecans on a baking sheet and place in the oven for 5 minutes, or until well toasted. Allow to cool a little, then roughly chop and set aside.

3 To make the pancake batter, whisk the flour, baking powder, and superfine sugar in a medium bowl. Make a well in the center, then add the egg, milk, melted butter, and salt and whisk together until smooth. Set aside until needed.

4 Peel and core the apples, then cut them into thick slices.

5 Place a large nonstick frying pan over medium-high heat and add 3½ tablespoons of the butter. When melted, add the apples and cook until they begin to brown, 2–3 minutes. Pour in the Calvados and carefully flambé it in the pan. When the flames die down, add the vanilla paste and brown sugar and mix well. Pour in the cream, stir well, then remove from the heat.

6 Place two nonstick frying pans over medium-high heat and rub with a little of the remaining butter. Add large spoonfuls of the batter to the pans, and cook for a minute or two on each side, until lightly browned. Transfer to a baking sheet and keep warm while you make the rest of the pancakes (there should be 12–16 small pancakes in total).

7 Put the apples back over high heat and cook until the caramel sauce thickens, 1–2 mintues.

8 Serve the pancakes in stacks of 3 or 4 on each plate. Top with apples and smother in caramel sauce. Sprinkle with the toasted pecans and serve with a big scoop of vanilla ice cream on the side.

Choc Nut Vegan Mousse

Serves 4–6

5 ounces ripe avocados

5 ounces bananas

1 tablespoon vanilla extract

2 tablespoons cold strong black coffee

3 tablespoons peanut butter

⅓ cup good-quality cocoa powder

⅓ cup maple syrup

Generous pinch of sea salt

6 tablespoons salted roasted peanuts,
  roughly chopped

Large handful of caramel popcorn,
  to serve

I know it sounds crazy to make a dessert with avocado, but if you want to create a vegan mousse that has a silky, creamy texture without using eggs or cream, a ripe avo is the perfect ingredient. It also has the added bonus of being extremely good for you, so this rich, indulgent chocolate pudding is guilt-free…well, almost.

1 Scoop the avocado flesh into a large food processor.

2 Peel the bananas, break them into large chunks, and add to the processor. Add the vanilla, coffee, peanut butter, cocoa powder, maple syrup, and salt and blend until smooth.

3 Taste the mousse and add a little more salt, as necessary.

4 Sprinkle in half the peanuts and blend for a few more seconds.

5 Spoon the mousse into small bowls and sprinkle with the remaining nuts. Crumble a few pieces of caramel popcorn over each bowl before serving.

Flourless Chocolate and Raspberry Pots

Serves 4

¾ cup dark chocolate chips (60–80% cocoa solids)

3 large eggs

⅔ cup superfine sugar

Seeds from 1 vanilla pod

¼ cup ground almonds

¼ cup good-quality cocoa powder, plus extra for dusting

6 ounces fresh raspberries, plus extra to serve

4 teaspoons crème de cacao or raspberry liqueur

These delicious mini chocolate–almond puddings have fresh raspberries steeped in liqueur hidden at the bottom of the pots for a boozy, fruity surprise. As they are made with ground almonds rather than flour, they are gluten free and have a dense, moist texture that I really love. Serve with a few extra fresh raspberries and a drizzle of cream for chocolate pudding perfection.

1 Preheat the oven to 400°F.

2 Bring a kettle of water to a boil.

3 Put the chocolate into a small heatproof bowl and place in the microwave. Heat on high for 20 seconds, then stir and return to the microwave for another 20 seconds. Repeat the heating and stirring until the chocolate has melted. Leave to cool.

4 Separate the eggs into two bowls. Add half the sugar to the whites and beat with a handheld electric mixer on medium-high until stiff peaks form, 3–4 minutes.

5 Add the remaining sugar and the vanilla seeds to the egg yolks. Beat with the electric mixer on medium-high until thick, pale yellow, and fluffy. Add the melted chocolate, ground almonds, cocoa powder, and a spoonful of the egg whites and beat until well combined. Gently fold in the remaining whites, being careful not to knock out all the air.

6 Divide the raspberries among four 7-ounce ramekins. Add a teaspoonful of liqueur to each one, then gently spoon the chocolate mixture evenly over the fruit.

7 Put all four ramekins into a small baking dish and pour in just enough boiling water to come 1 inch up the sides. Place on the middle shelf of the oven and bake until slightly puffed and dry on top, 12–15 minutes.

8 When ready, serve immediately with a dusting of cocoa powder and a few extra raspberries.

Dark Chocolate and Coffee Mousse

Serves 4–6

10½ ounces dark chocolate (70% cocoa solids)

1¼ cups heavy cream

½ cup warm black coffee

6 egg yolks

1 tablespoon honey

3 tablespoons chocolate-coated coffee beans, lightly crushed, to serve

If you have more time...
...allow these mousses to set in the fridge for an hour before serving.

This is the perfect ending to a great meal—an after-dinner coffee and chocolate rolled into one! If you like things particularly dark and bitter, leave out the honey, or add a little extra if you prefer things sweeter. The mousse is delicious served immediately while still warm, but you can also put it in the fridge to allow it to cool and set.

1 Bring half a kettle of water to a boil. Pour it into a medium saucepan and bring to a very gentle simmer.

2 Break the chocolate into pieces and place in a medium heatproof bowl. Sit the bowl over the pan without it actually touching the water and allow the chocolate to melt. Set aside.

3 Pour the cream into another bowl and whisk to soft peaks, 3–4 minutes.

4 Put the coffee, egg yolks, and honey into a second heatproof bowl and whisk them together. Once combined, place the bowl over the pan of hot water and continue to whisk over low heat until the mixture thickens like custard, 3–4 minutes.

5 Whisk in the melted chocolate, then allow to cool for 5 minutes.

6 Gently fold in the cream until just incorporated.

7 The warm mousse can be served immediately, or poured into individual bowls and chilled to serve later.

8 Sprinkle some of the crushed coffee beans over each bowl before serving.

Tiramisu Pots

Serves 6

2 cups cold black coffee

¼ cup coffee liqueur

18 ladyfingers

1½ ounces dark chocolate (80% cocoa solids), for grating

1 tablespoon good-quality cocoa powder, for dusting

For the mascarpone cream

9 ounces mascarpone cheese

¼ cup condensed milk

1 cup heavy cream

½ cup Marsala wine

If you have more time...

...put these pots into the fridge for an hour or two before serving; the flavors really come together and they will be even more delicious.

For this cheat's tiramisu, I use condensed milk in the mascarpone cream rather than eggs, which would be more traditional but also more time-consuming. The milk brings a silky sweetness that goes beautifully with the coffee and chocolate, and it still ticks all the right tiramisu boxes for texture and flavor. If you're entertaining, make these ahead of time and leave them in the fridge until you are ready to serve.

1 Pour the coffee into a shallow tray and mix in the coffee liqueur. Carefully place the tray in the freezer.

2 Meanwhile, put the mascarpone and condensed milk into a medium bowl and whisk until smooth.

3 Put the cream in a separate bowl and beat with a handheld electric mixer until firm peaks form. Stir in the Marsala, then fold the cream into the mascarpone mixture.

4 Remove the coffee from the freezer. If it's still not cold, add a couple of ice cubes to the tray and stir until cool. Take 9 of the ladyfingers and soak them one at a time in the coffee for a few seconds. Break the soaked ladyfingers in half and divide them among the bottoms of six serving glasses.

5 Using a fine grater and half of the chocolate, grate a layer of chocolate directly over the ladyfingers. Spoon half the mascarpone mixture among the glasses.

6 Dip the remaining ladyfingers into the coffee one at a time. Break them in half and divide among the glasses. Grate the rest of the chocolate over the ladyfingers, then top each glass with the remaining mascarpone mixture.

7 Before serving, use a small tea strainer to dust cocoa powder over the surface.

Index

Acknowledgments

However fast the recipes are, it still takes a great deal of time and effort to produce a new cookbook. I am, therefore, hugely grateful to the brilliant people at Hodder & Stoughton for helping me pull this one together with their customary enthusiasm, patience, and dedication. Particular thanks go to editorial director Nicky Ross, project editor Natalie Bradley, art director Alasdair Oliver, and senior production controller Susan Spratt for creating the book and to Caitriona Horne and Jenny Platt for marketing and publicizing it. It has been great working with you all again. Editorially, thanks so much to Camilla Stoddart and Trish Burgess for helping me dot my i's and cross my t's—you've done a great job.

Thanks also to my publishers for putting together a winning creative team to make the book look so beautiful. I am hugely thankful to Peter Dawson and Alice Kennedy-Owen at Grade Design for the skillful art direction and beautiful design; Louise Hagger for the stunning photography; Nicole Herft for the knockout food styling and for her amazing attitude to hard work; and Alexander Breeze and Louie Waller for their wizardry with the props.

Thank you to James "Jocky" Petrie and all the chefs in my restaurants who work tirelessly to push the boundaries of food development. I really appreciate everything you do.

I am so grateful to Rachel Ferguson in the UK and Katie Besozzi in the US for helping me keep to my busy schedule on both sides of the pond. I don't know where I'd be without you. Literally!

Lastly, I'd like to thank my incredible family: my wonderful wife, Tana, and our five children, Megan, Holly, Jack, Tilly, and new arrival Oscar. You lot are everything to me and I am grateful every day.

Imperial/Metric Conversion Chart

All equivalents are rounded, for practical convenience.

Weight

1 oz	25g
2 oz	50g
3½ oz	100g
5 oz	150g
7 oz	200g
9 oz	250g
10 oz	300g
14 oz	400g
1 lb 2 oz	500g
2¼ lb	1 kg

Volume (liquids)

1 tsp	—	5ml
1 tbsp	—	15ml
⅛ cup	1 fl oz	30ml
¼ cup	2 fl oz	60ml
⅓ cup	—	75ml
½ cup	4 fl oz	120ml
⅔ cup	5 fl oz	150ml
¾ cup	—	175ml
1 cup	8 fl oz	250ml
4 cups	1 quart	1 litre

Length

½ inch	1cm
1 inch	2.5cm
8 inches	20cm
10 inches	25cm
12 inches	30cm

Oven temperatures

Fahrenheit	Celsius
275	140
300	150
325	160
350	180
375	190
400	200
425	220
450	230

Volume (dry ingredients—an approximate guide)

butter	1 cup (2 sticks)	225g
rolled oats	1 cup	100g
fine powders (e.g., flour)	1 cup	125g
breadcrumbs (fresh)	1 cup	50g
breadcrumbs (dried)	1 cup	125g
nuts (e.g., almonds)	1 cup	125g
seeds (e.g., chia)	1 cup	160g
dried fruit (e.g., raisins)	1 cup	150g
dried legumes (large, e.g., chickpeas)	1 cup	170g
grains, granular goods, and small dried legumes (e.g., rice, quinoa, sugar, lentils)	1 cup	200g
grated cheese	1 cup	100g